WOW HITS 2007

SONGBOOK

30 OF THE YEAR'S TOP CHRISTIAN ARTISTS AND HITS

SONGBOOK

30 OF THE YEAR'S TOP CHRISTIAN ARTISTS AND HITS

WOW HITS 2007 recorded on Sparrow CD #SPD67196

Edited by

BRYCE INMAN & KEN BARKER

Transcribed by

BRYCE INMAN, JARED HASCHEK & RIC SIMENSON

WOWHITS 2007
CONTENTS

Lifesong

Recorded by Casting Crowns

Words and Music by
MARK HALL

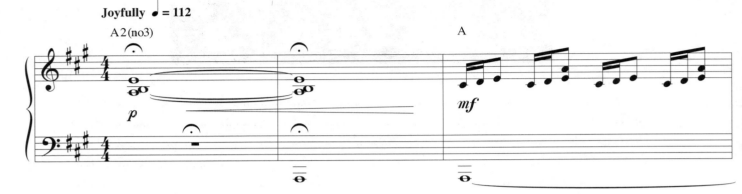

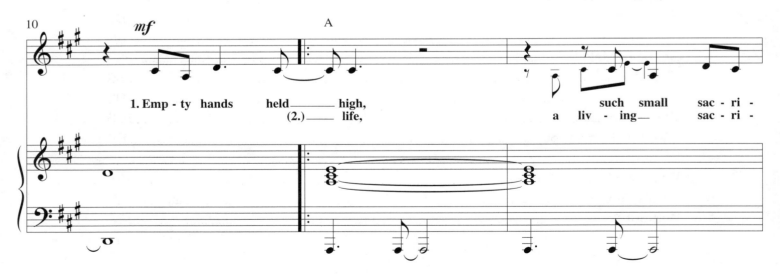

1. Emp - ty hands held_____ high,
(2.)_____ life,

such small sac - ri -
a liv - ing_____ sac - ri -

You. Let my life - song sing to You.—

Let my life - song

sing to You.—— I wan - na

sign Your— name— to the end of— this day, know-in' that my heart— was

true. Let my life - song sing to You.—

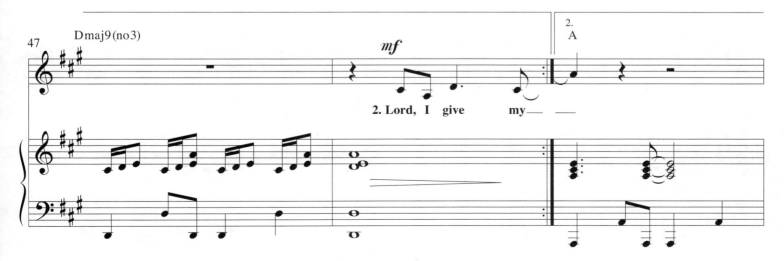

2. Lord, I give my— —

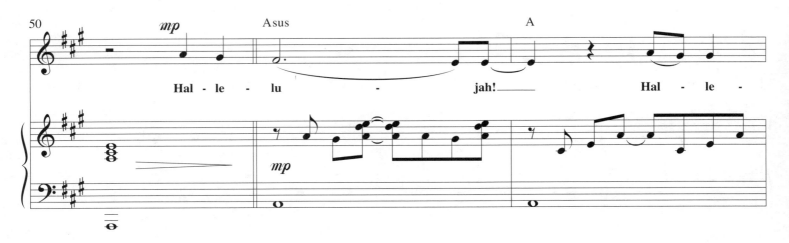

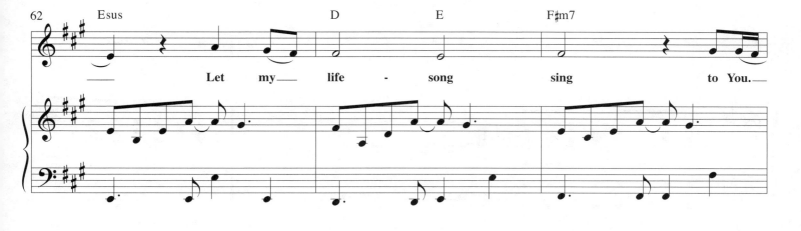

13

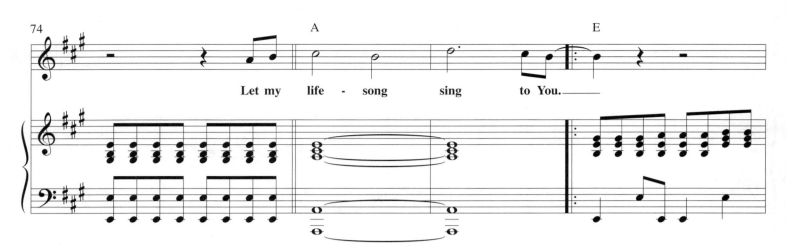

Let my life - song sing to You. ____

Let my life - song sing to You. ____

____ I wan-na sign Your ____ name ____ to the

end of ____ this day, know-in' that my heart ____ was true. Let my

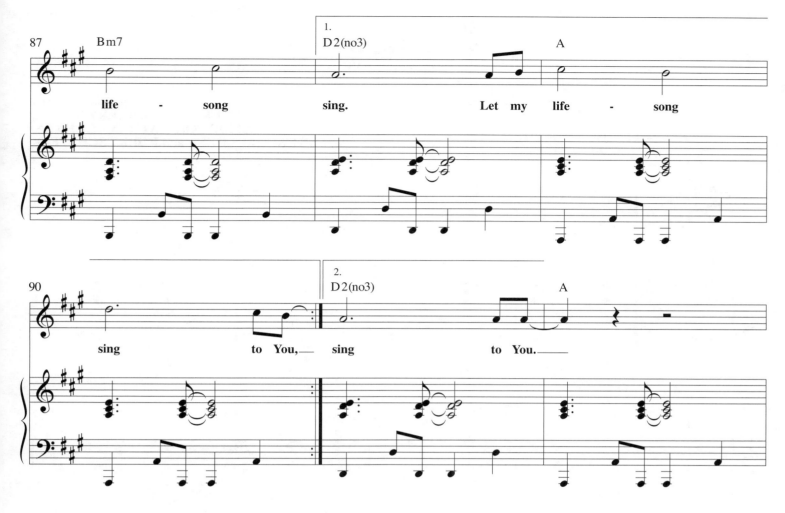

life - song sing. Let my life - song

sing to You, sing to You.

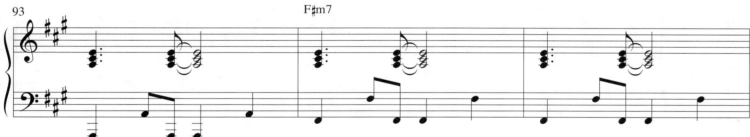

So Long Self

Recorded by MercyMe

Words and Music by
**BART MILLARD, BARRY GRAUL,
JIM BRYSON, NATHAN COCHRAN,
MIKE SCHEUCHZER and ROBBY SCHAFFER**

1. Well if I come_____ a - cross_____ a lit -
2. _____ Stop right there_____ be - cause_____ I know_____

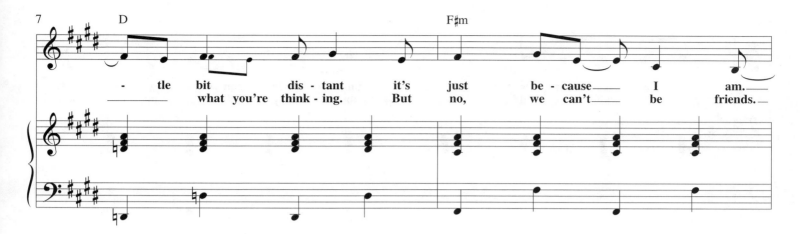

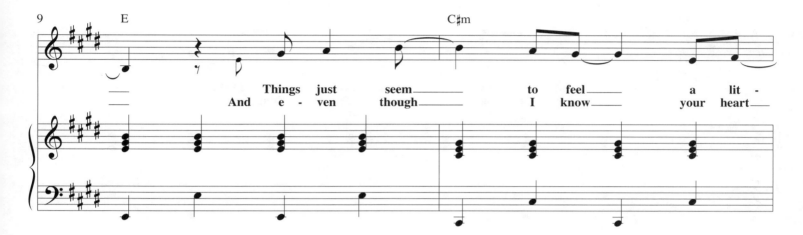

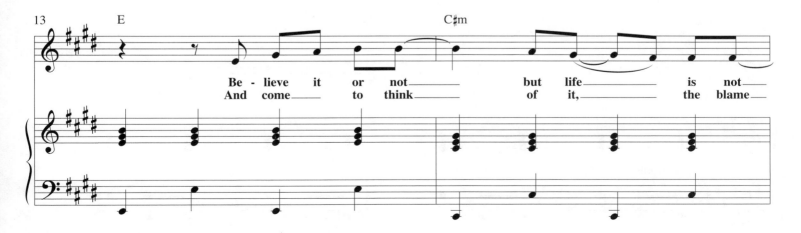

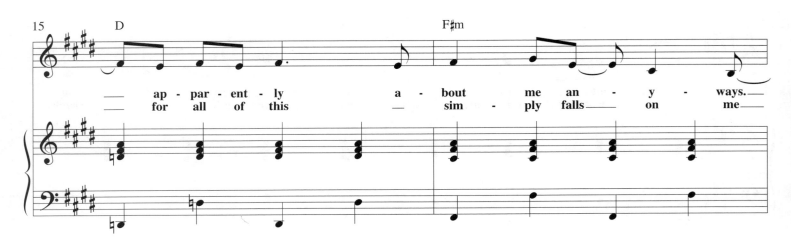

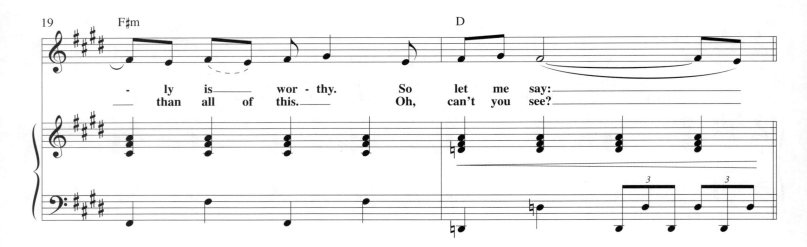

but I____ have found____ some - bod - y else.____

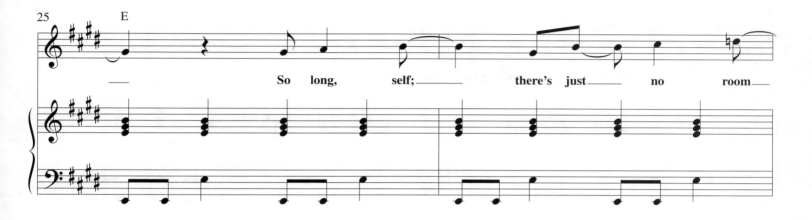

So long, self;____ there's just____ no room____

for two,____ so you____ are gon - na have to move.____

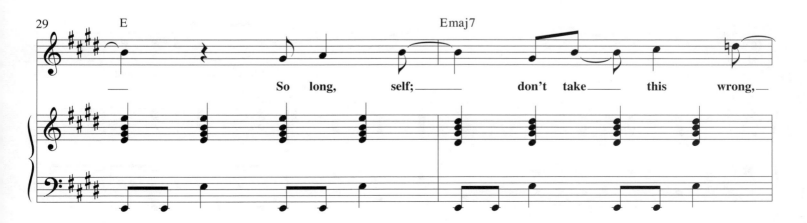

So long, self;____ don't take____ this wrong,____

but you___ are wrong___ for me.___ Fare - well,___

3rd time to CODA ⊕

___ oh well,___ good - bye,___ don't cry,___

1.

Oh,_____ so long, self.___

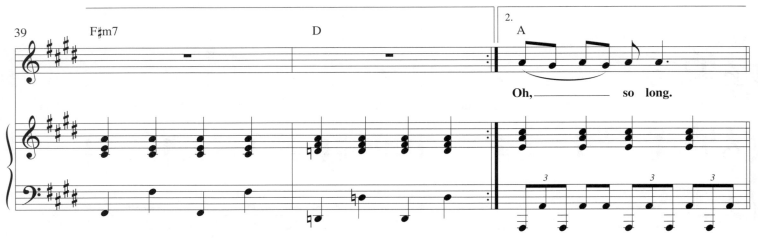

2.

Oh,_____ so long.

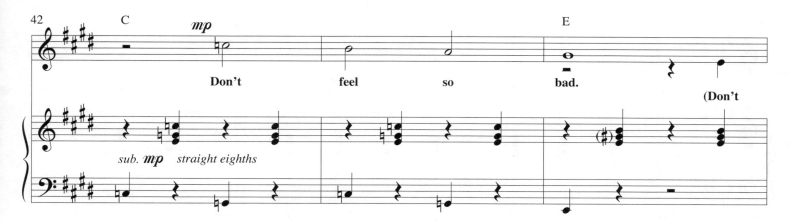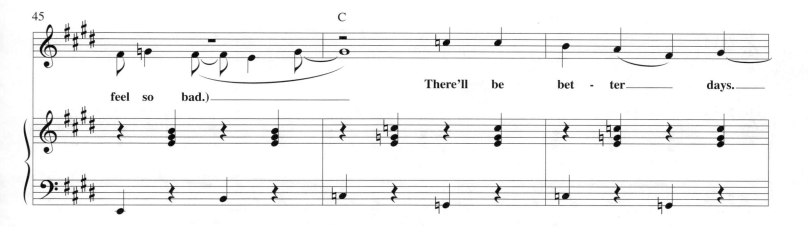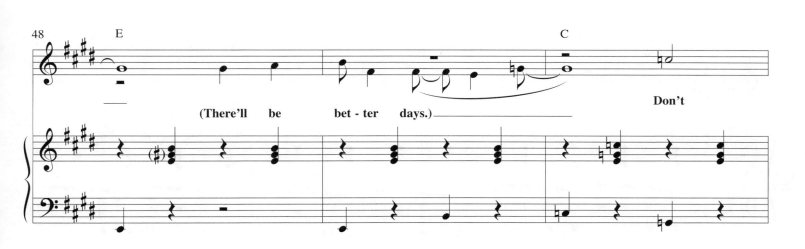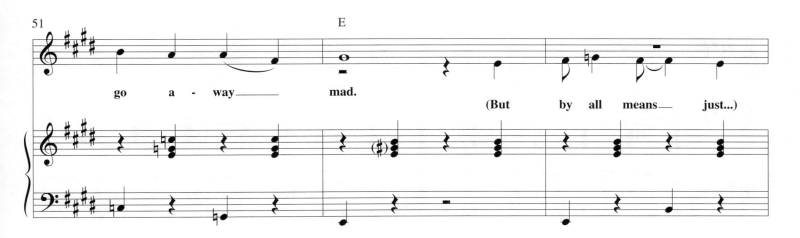

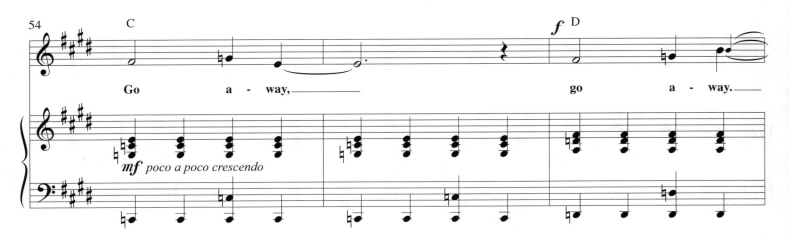

Go a - way,_____ go a - way.___

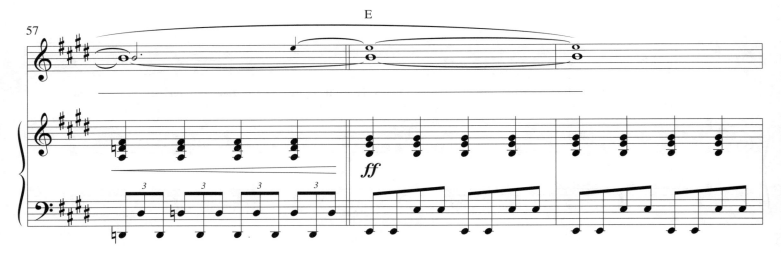

D.S. al CODA 𝄋

⊕ CODA

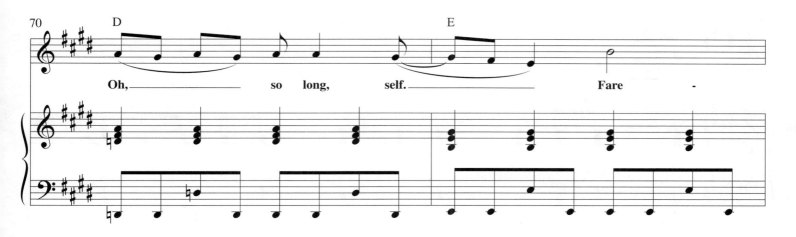

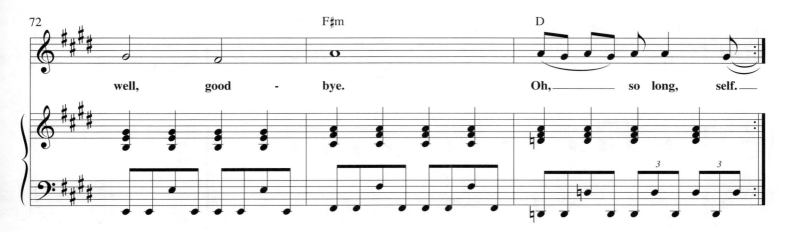

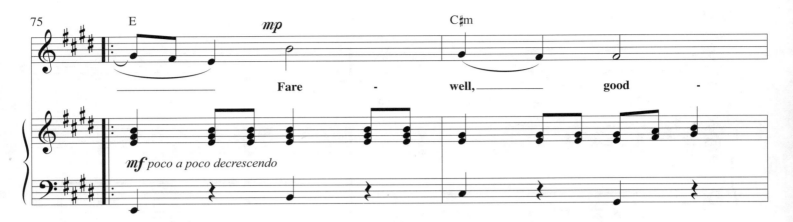

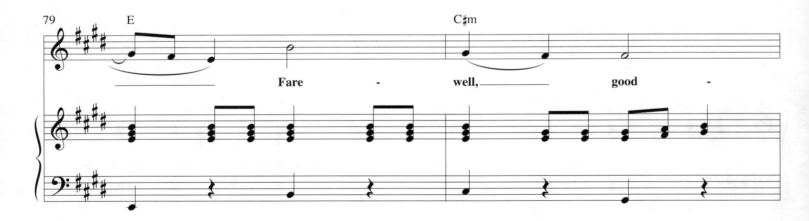

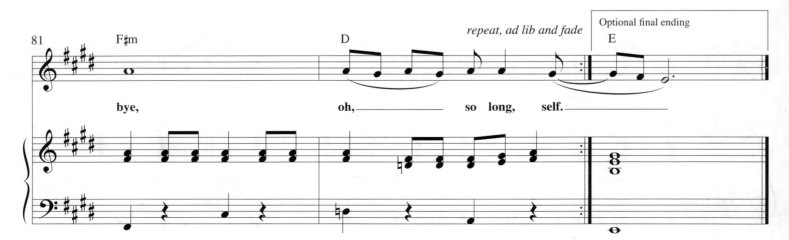

How Great Is Our God

Recorded by Chris Tomlin

Words and Music by
CHIRS TOMLIN, JESSE REEVES
and ED CASH

With praise ♩ = 76

Sing top stave 1st and 2nd times only
Optional: 5th time a cappella

Name a - bove all names,

How great is our God!

Wor - thy of all praise.

Sing with me: How great is our God!

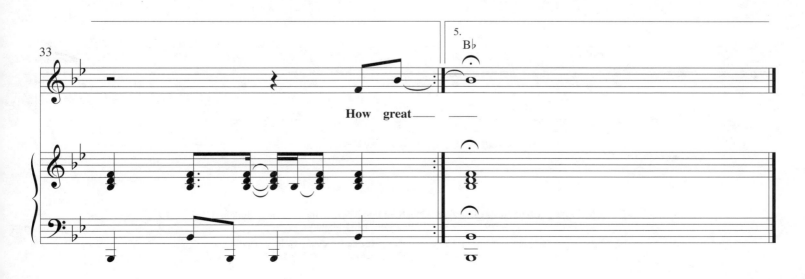

My Savior, My God

Recorded by Aaron Shust

Words and Music by
AARON SHUST

Sav - ior.

2. I take Him at His word and

deed,
(3.) bring

Christ died to save me, this I
my strength, my sol - ace from this

read,
spring

and in my heart I find a
that He who lives to be my

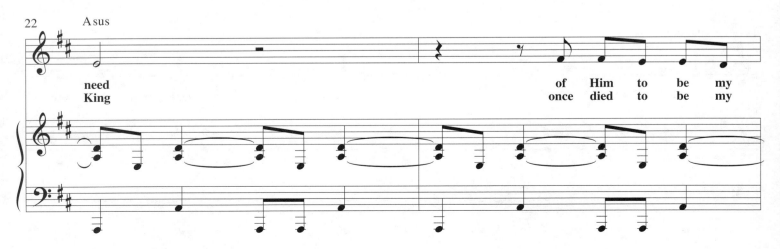

need
King

of Him to be my
once died to be my

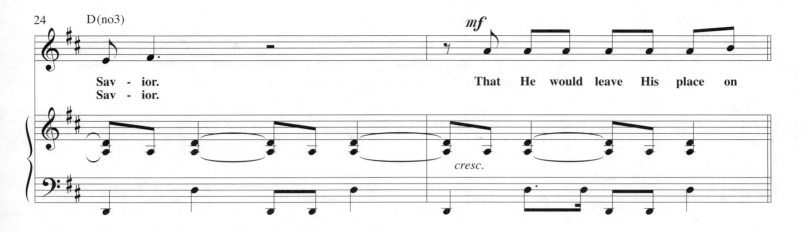

Sav - ior. That He would leave His place on

Sav - ior.

high and come for sin - ful man to

die. You count it strange, so once did

I _____ be - fore I knew my

al - ways gon - na be._____

1.

2.

3. Yes, liv - ing, dy - ing, let me

mf guitar solo

al - ways there for me.___ My God He was,___ my God He is,___ my God He's

al - ways gon - na be. My Sav - ior lives,___ my Sav - ior loves,___ my Sav - ior lives,

___ my Sav - ior loves,___ my Sav - ior lives.___

This Man

Recorded by Jeremy Camp

Words and Music by
JEREMY CAMP

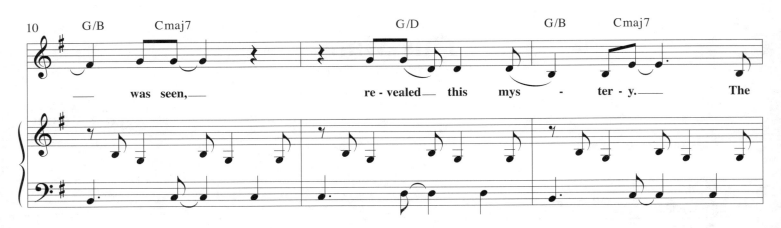

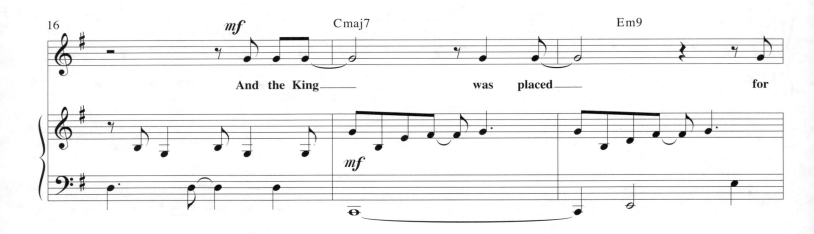

from— this place._____

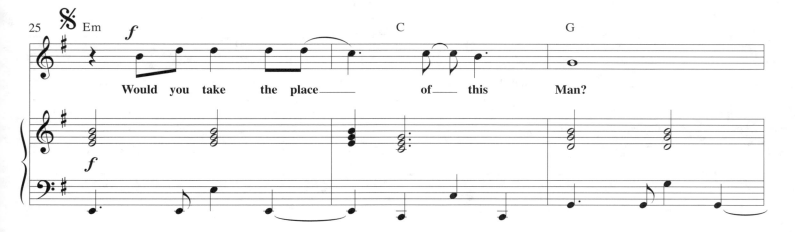

Would you take the place____ of— this Man?

Would you take the nails____ from— His hands?—

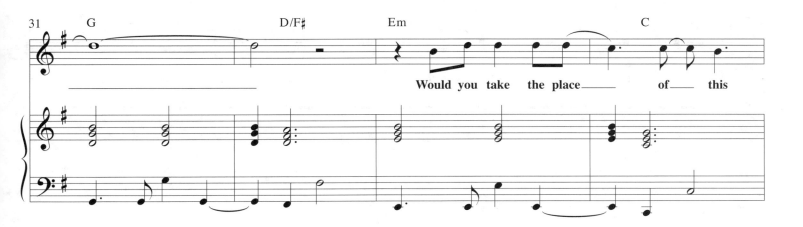

Would you take the place____ of— this

Man?   Would you take   the nails—

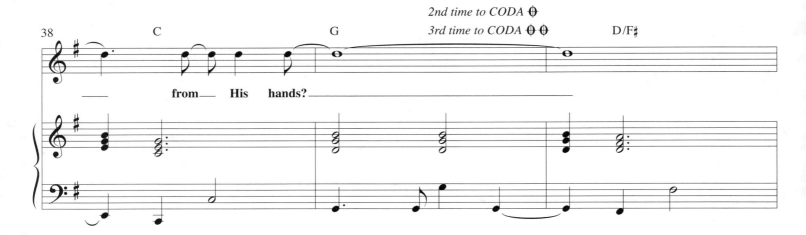

2nd time to CODA ⊕
3rd time to CODA ⊕ ⊕

—   from— His   hands?—

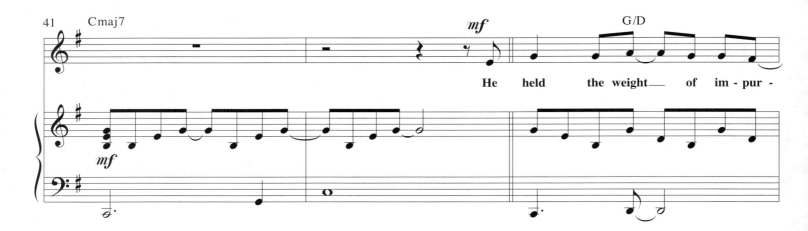

He   held   the weight—   of   im - pur -

- i - ty—   the Fa - ther   would— not   see.—   The

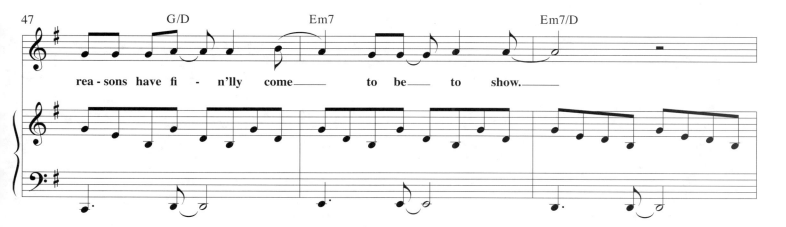

rea - sons have fi - n'lly come——— to be——— to show.———

The depth——— of——— His grace———

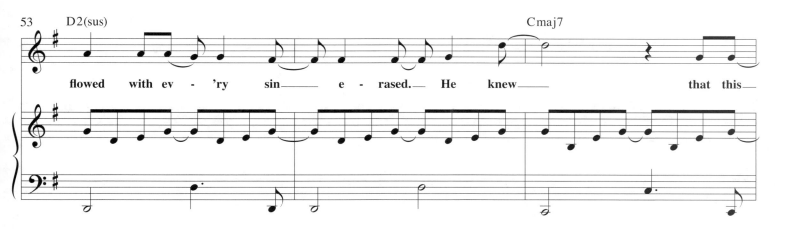

flowed with ev - 'ry sin——— e - rased.——— He knew——— that this———

——— was why——— He came.———

D.S. al CODA 𝄉

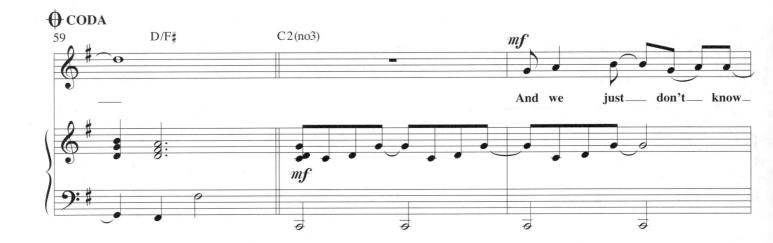

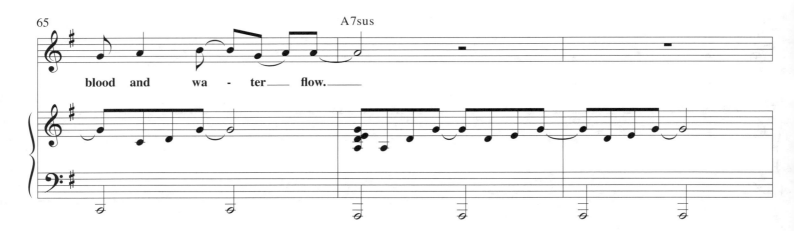

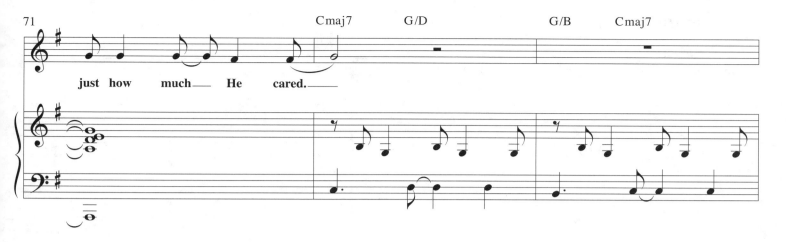

just how much— He cared.—

And the veil——— was torn—

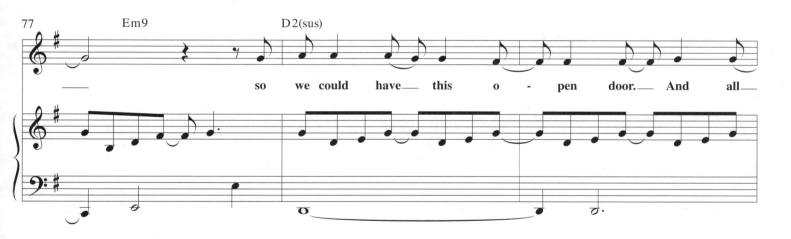

— so we could have— this o - pen door. And all—

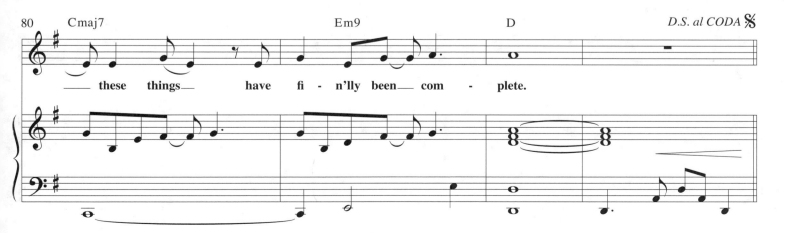

D.S. al CODA 𝄋

— these things— have fi - n'lly been— com - plete.

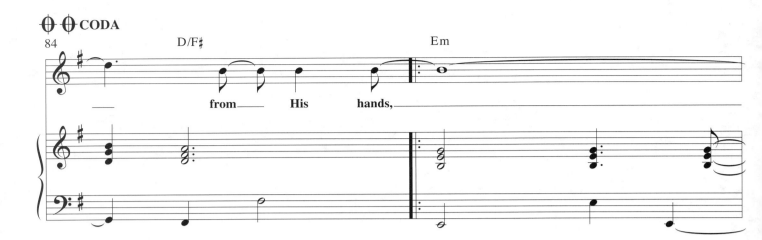

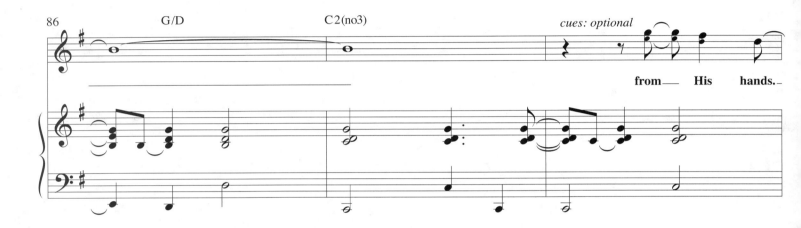

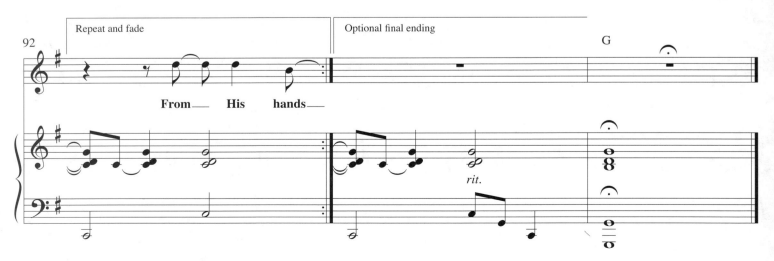

Held

Recorded by Natalie Grant

Words and Music by
CHRISTA WELLS

Slow four, with emotion ♩. = 66

Two months is too lit - tle; they let him go.___ They had no___ sud - den heal - ing. To think that prov - i - dence___ would

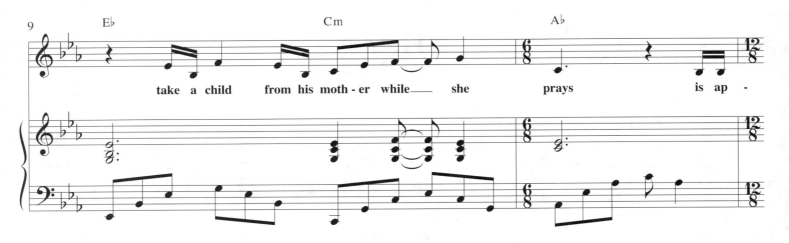

take a child from his moth - er while___ she prays is ap -

pall - ing._____ Who told us we'd be res - cued?

What has changed and___ why should we be saved_____ from night - mares?_____

We're ask - ing why this hap - pens to us who have died___ to___

live. It's un-fair. This is what it

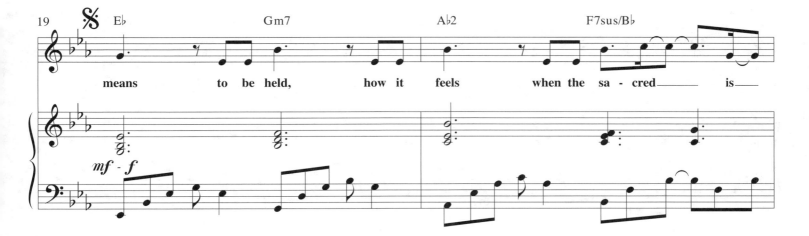

means to be held, how it feels when the sa-cred is

torn from your life and you sur-vive. This is what it

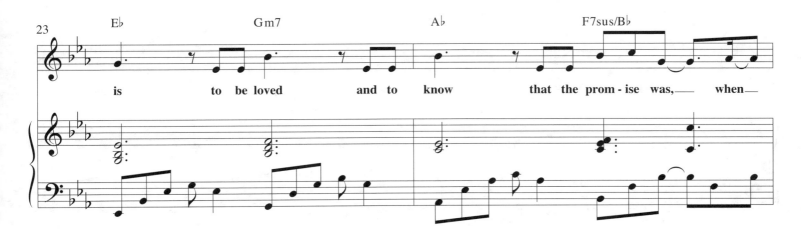

is to be loved and to know that the prom-ise was, when

ev - 'ry - thing—— fell, we'd be held.——————

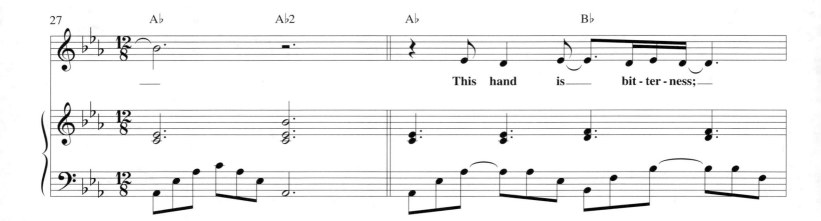

This hand is—— bit - ter - ness;——

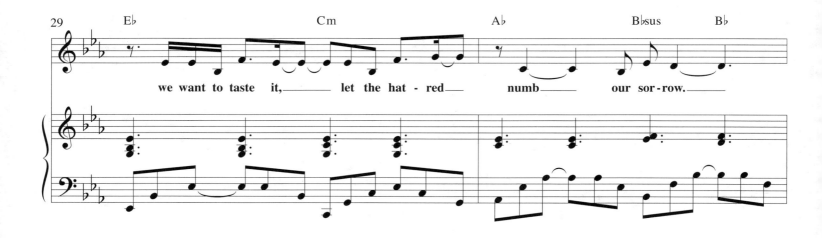

we want to taste it,—— let the hat - red—— numb—— our sor - row.——

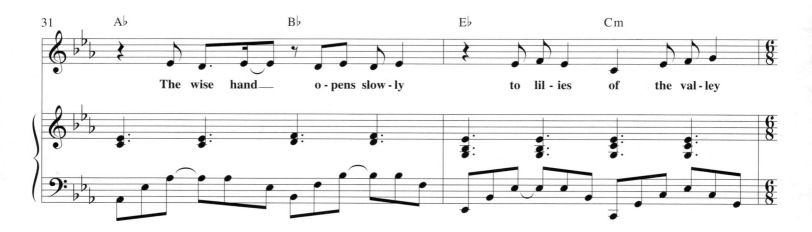

The wise hand—— o - pens slow - ly to lil - ies of the val - ley

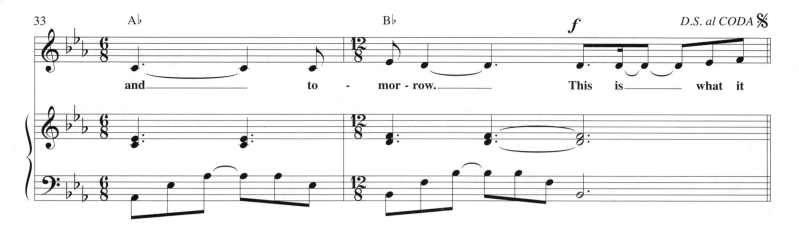

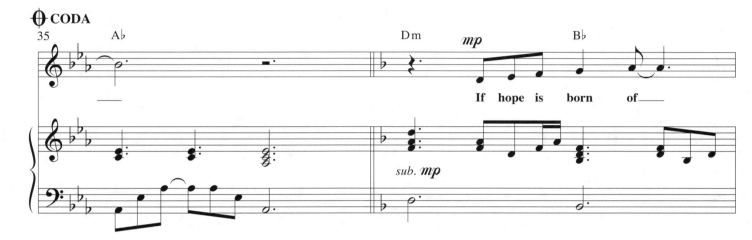

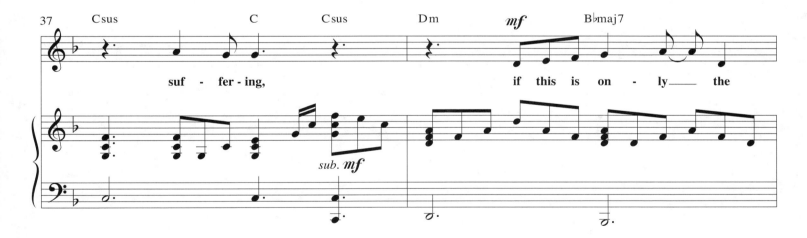

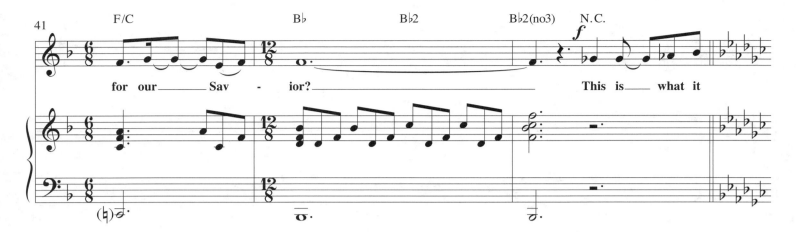

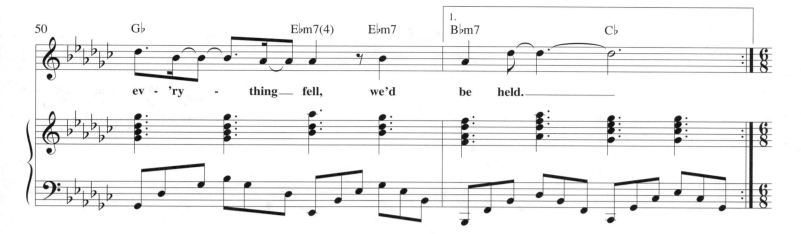

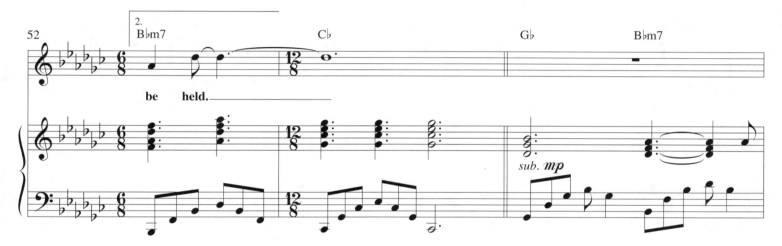

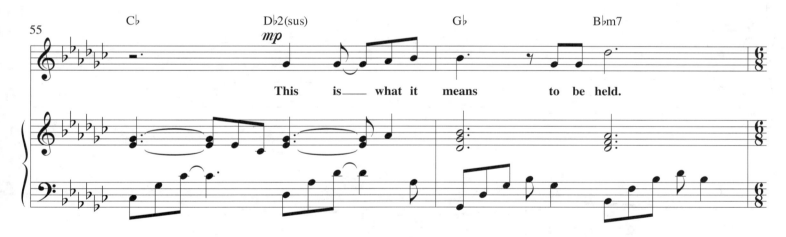

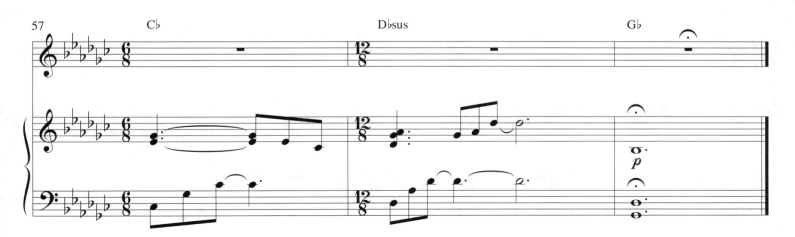

Cry Out to Jesus

Recorded by Third Day

Words and Music by
DAVID CARR, BRAD AVERY,
TAI ANDERSON, MARK LEE
and MAC POWELL

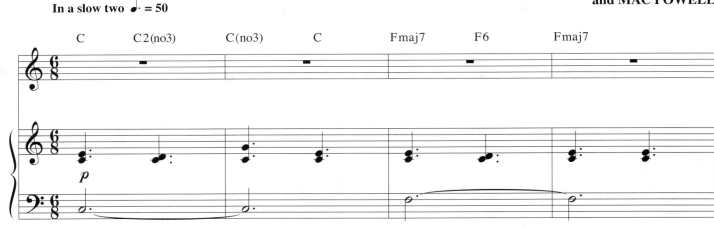

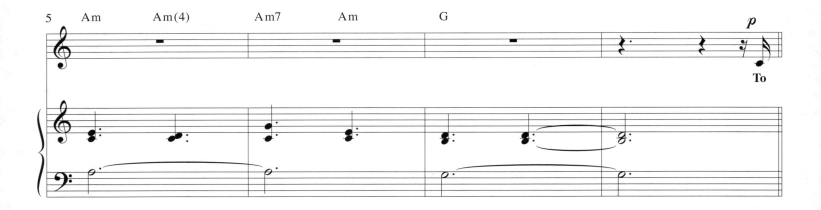

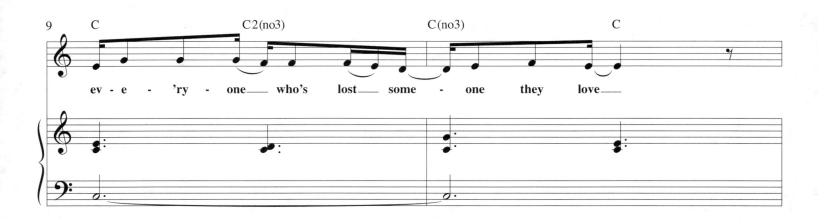

ev - e - 'ry - one who's lost some - one they love

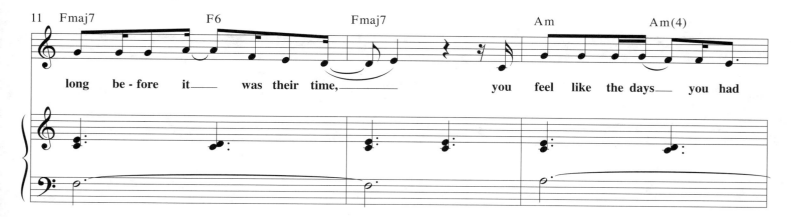

long be - fore it___ was their time,_____ you feel like the days___ you had

were not e - nough___ when you said___ good - bye. And to

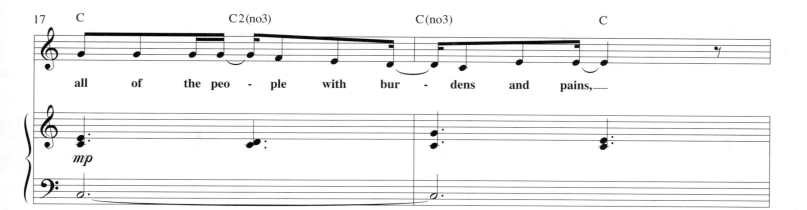

all of the peo - ple with bur - dens and pains,___

keep - ing you back___ from your life,_____ you be -

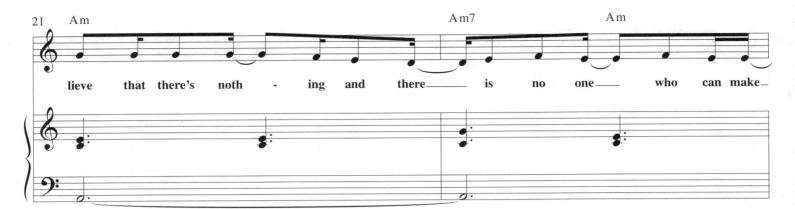

lieve that there's noth - ing and there_____ is no one_____ who can make_____

_____ it right.   And there is   hope   for   the   help - less,_____

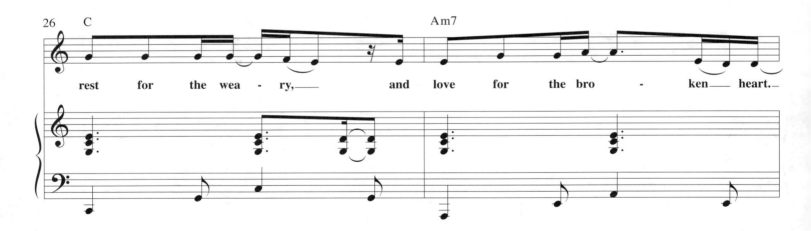

rest   for   the   wea - ry,_____   and   love   for   the   bro - ken_____ heart.

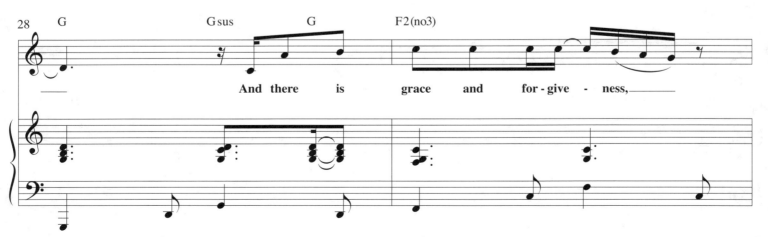

_____   And   there   is   grace   and   for - give - ness,_____

30 C ... Am7 ... *2nd time to CODA*

mer - cy and heal - ing.___ He'll meet you wher - ev - er you___ are.___

32 G ... F ... Fmaj7 ... F6 ... Fmaj7

___ Cry out to Je - sus,___ cry out to___

35 C ... Dm7 ... C/E ... F2(no3) ... Am ... G

Je - sus.___ For the

38 C ... C2(no3) ... C

mar - riage that's strug - gl - ing___ just___ to hang on,___ they've

lost all of their— faith in love,— and they've

done all they can— to make it— right a - gain,— still it's not

e - nough.— For the ones who can't break— the ad - dic -

- tions and— chains; you try to give up,— but you come—

back____ a - gain.____ Just re - mem - ber that you're____ not a - lone____

____ in your shame____ and your suf - fer - ing._____ There is

D.S. al CODA

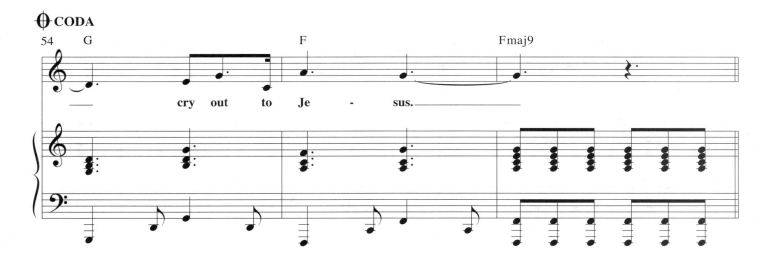

CODA

cry out to Je - sus._____

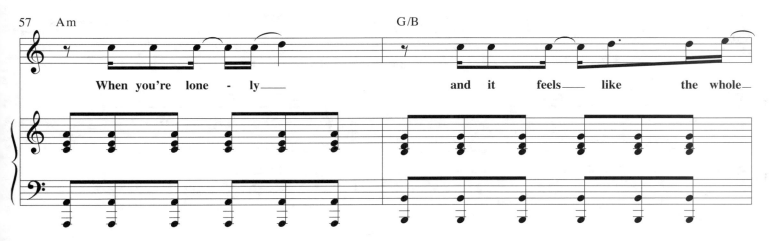

When you're lone - ly____ and it feels____ like the whole____

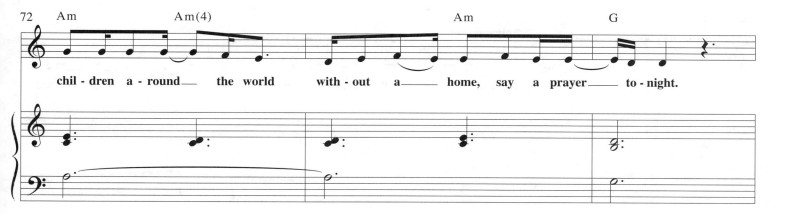

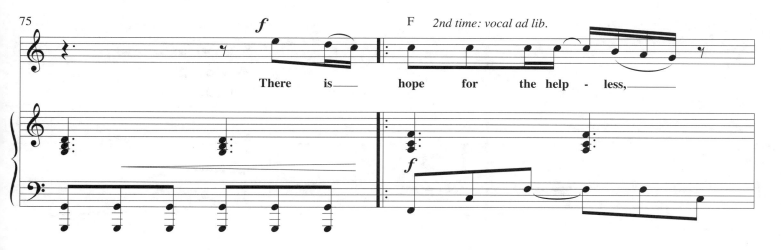

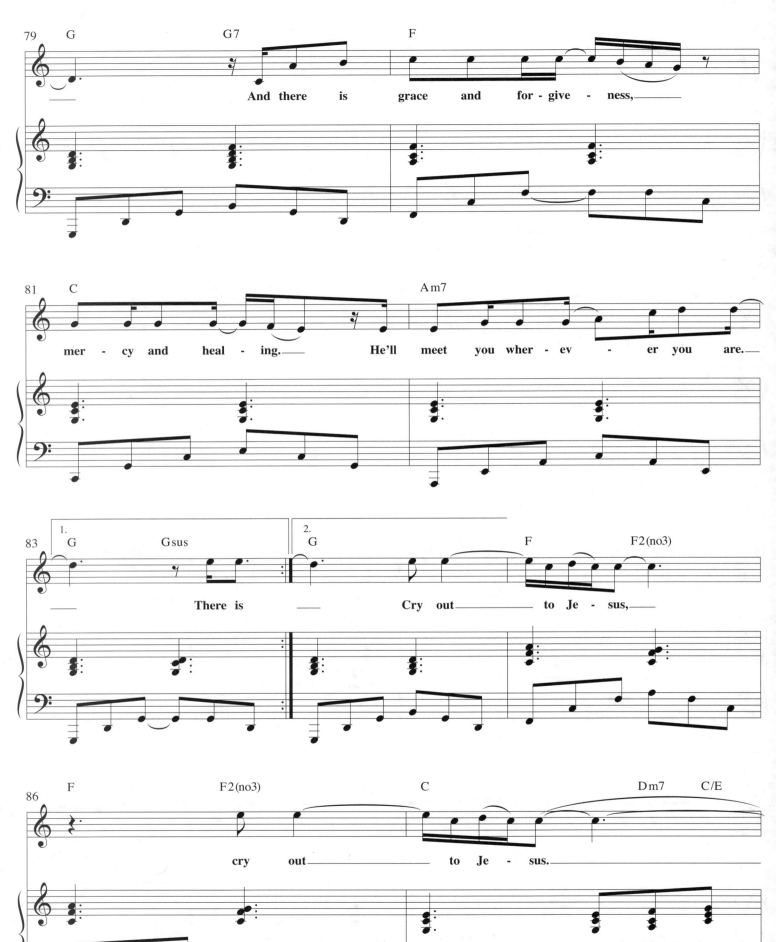

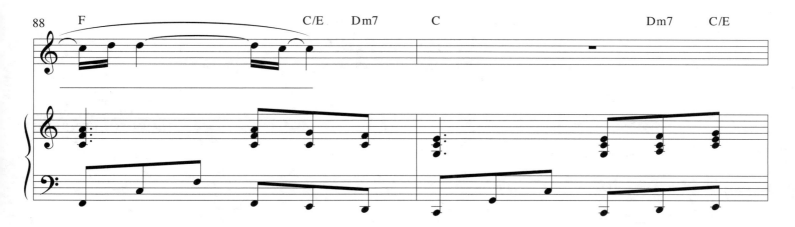

Oh,_____ cry out_____ to Je - sus,_____

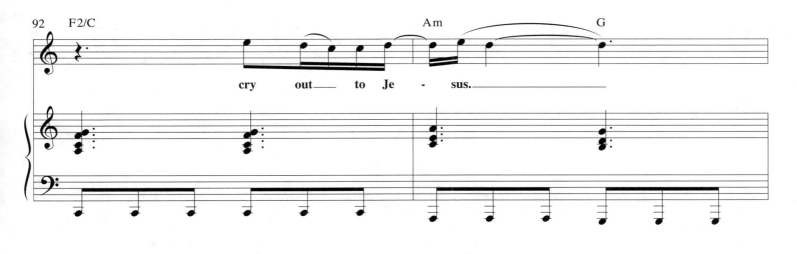

cry out_____ to Je - sus._____

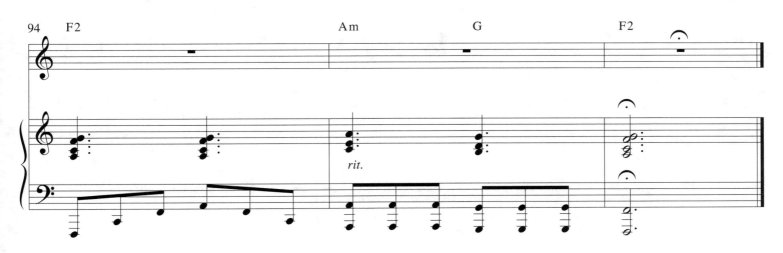

rit.

Only Grace

Recorded by Matthew West

Words and Music by
MATTHEW WEST and
KENNY GREENBERG

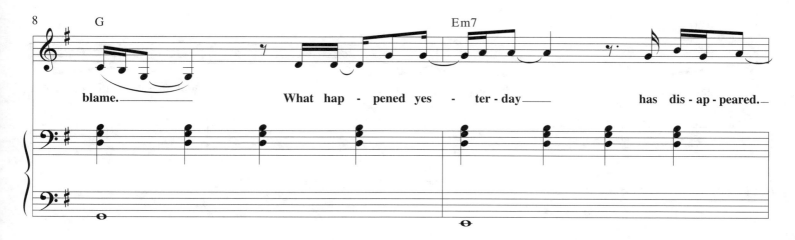

blame._____ What hap - pened yes - ter - day_____ has dis - ap - peared._

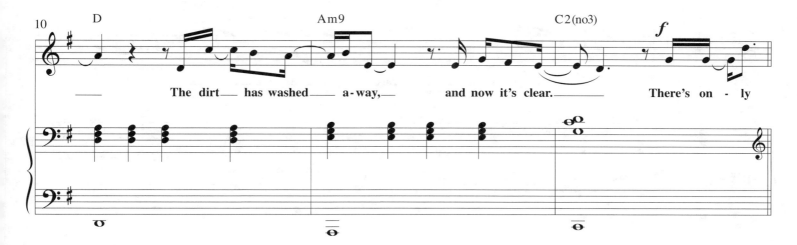

___ The dirt___ has washed___ a - way,___ and now it's clear._____ There's on - ly

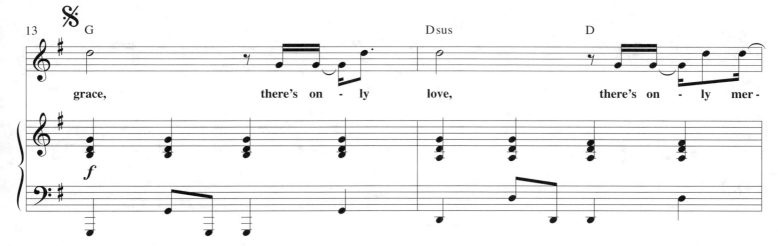

grace, there's on - ly love, there's on - ly mer -

- cy, and___ be - lieve___ me, it's e - nough._____ Your sins___ are

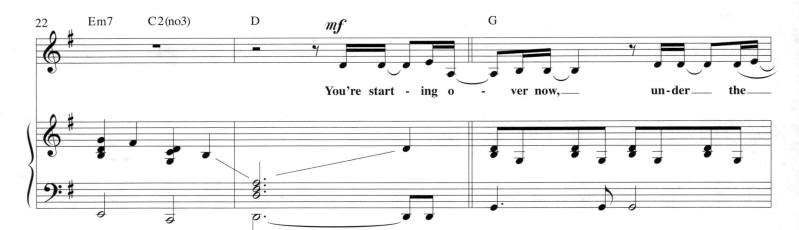

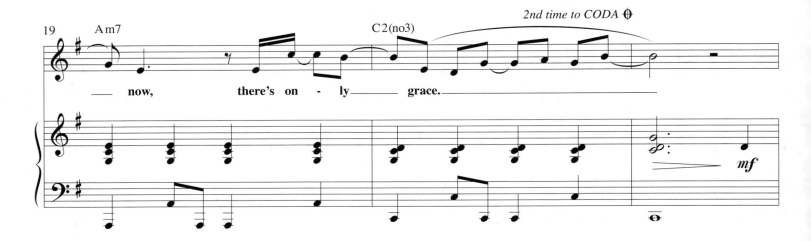

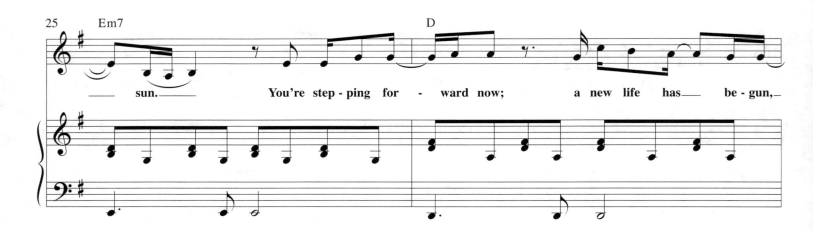

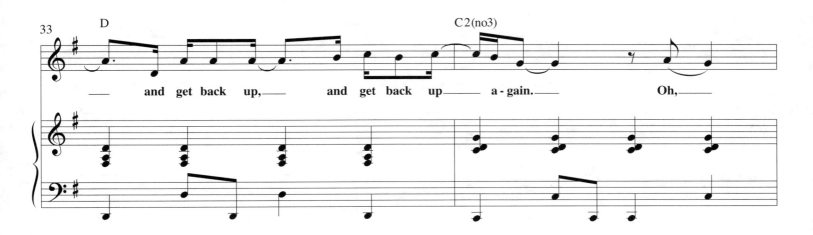

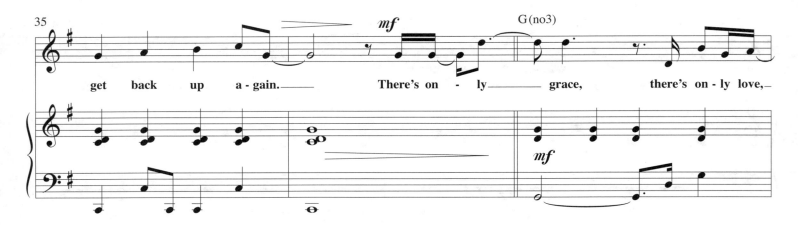

get back up a - gain._____ There's on - ly_____ grace, there's on - ly love,_____

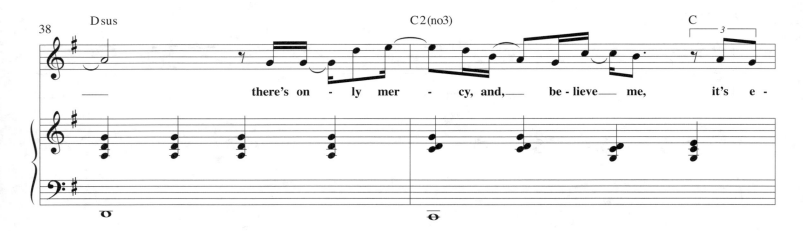

_____ there's on - ly mer - cy, and,_____ be - lieve_____ me, it's e -

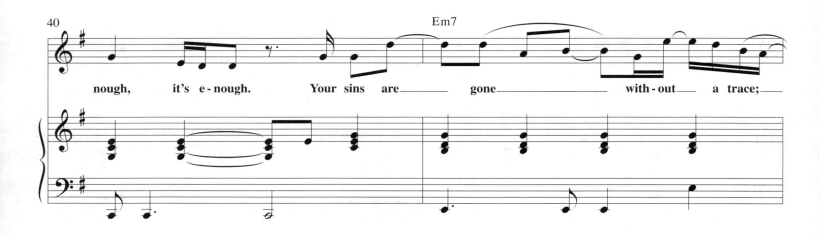

nough, it's e - nough. Your sins are_____ gone_____ with - out_____ a trace;_____

_____ and there's noth - ing left_____ now, there's on - ly,

there's on - ly_____ grace._____

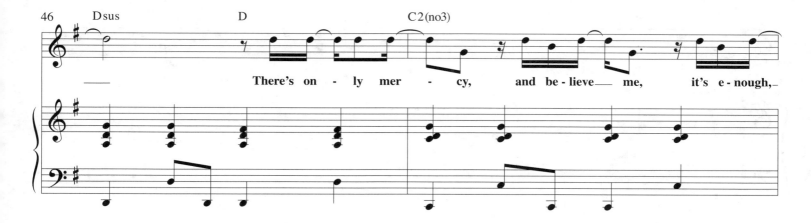

_____ There's on - ly mer - cy, and be - lieve_ me, it's e - nough,_

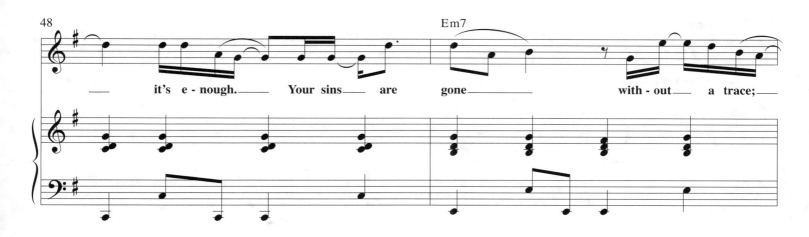

_____ it's e - nough._____ Your sins_ are gone_____ with - out_ a trace;_____

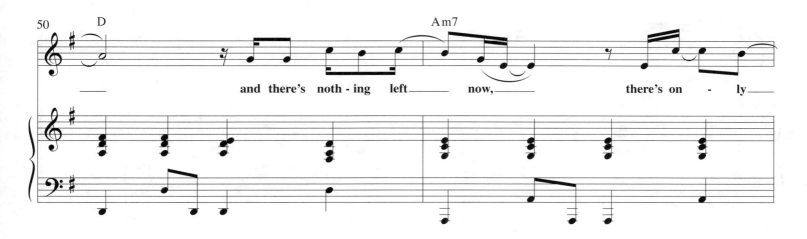

_____ and there's noth - ing left_____ now,_____ there's on - ly_____

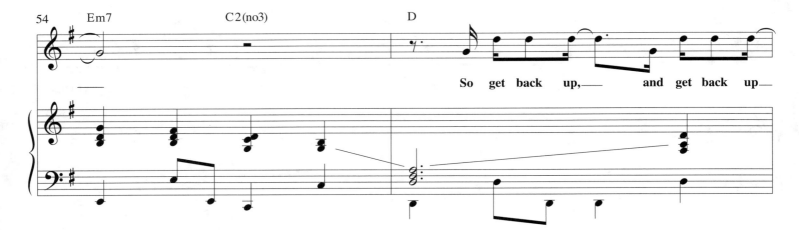

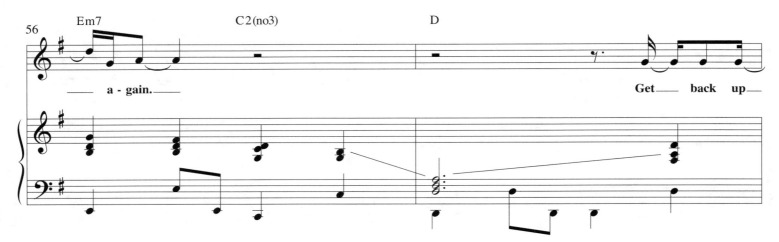

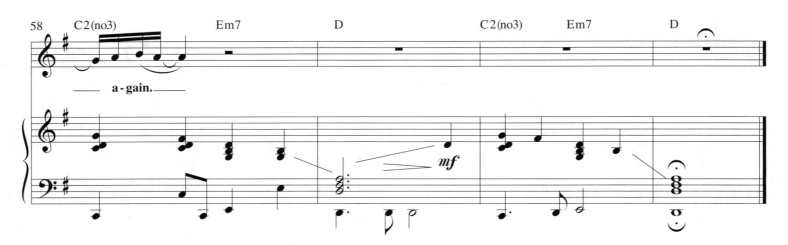

Wholly Yours

Recorded by the David Crowder Band

Words and Music by
DAVID CROWDER

With praise ♩ = 76

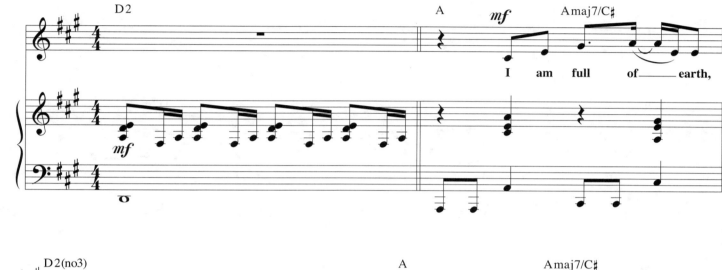

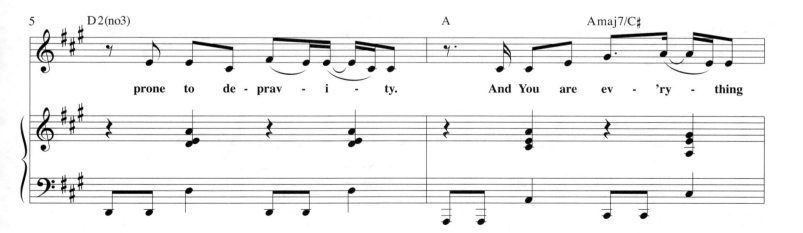

that is bright and__ clean.__ The an - to - nym of __ me,

You are di - vin - i - ty. What a cer - tain sign__ of

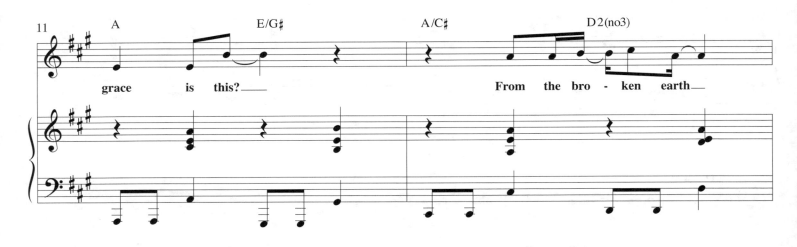

grace is this?__ From the bro - ken earth__

flow - ers come__ up, push - ing through__ the dirt.__ You are ho -

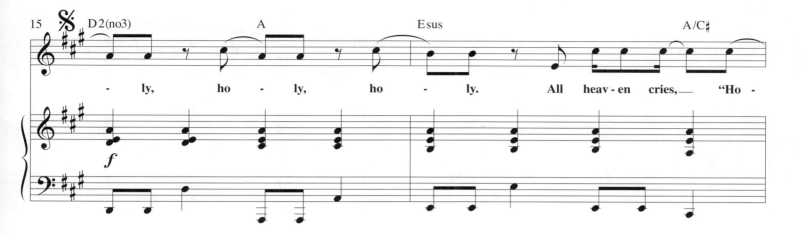

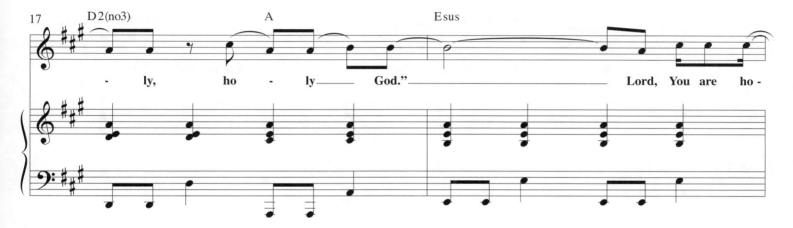

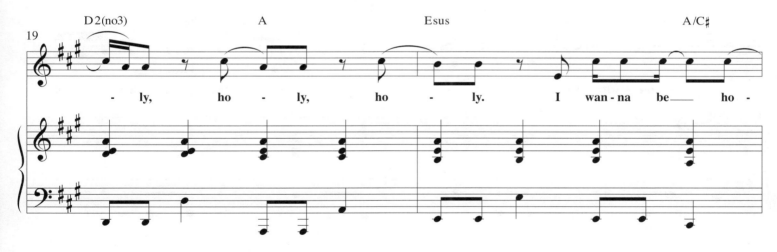

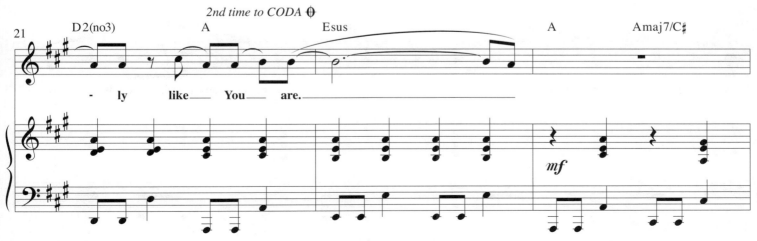

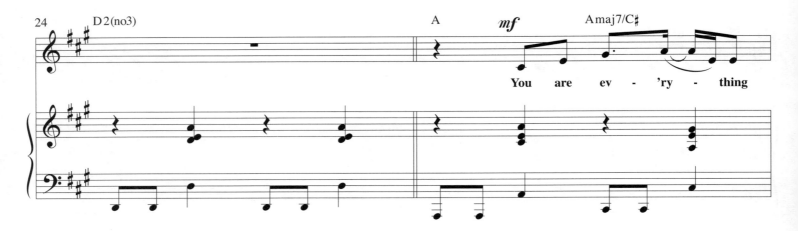

You are ev - 'ry - thing

that is bright and___ clean, and You're cov - er - ing

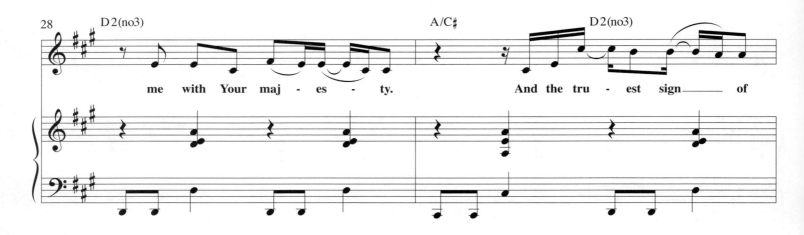

me with Your maj - es - ty. And the tru - est sign___ of

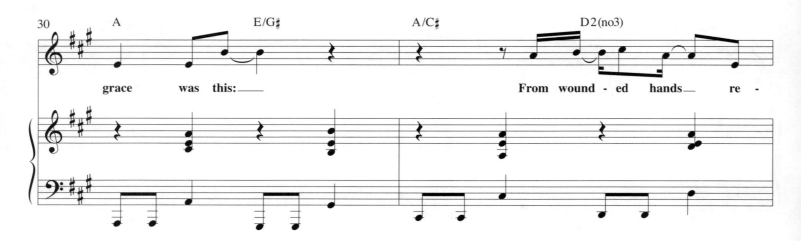

grace was this:___ From wound - ed hands___ re -

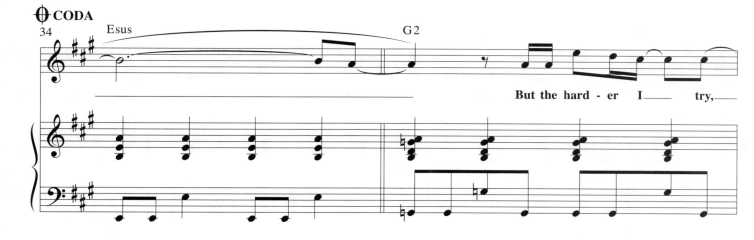

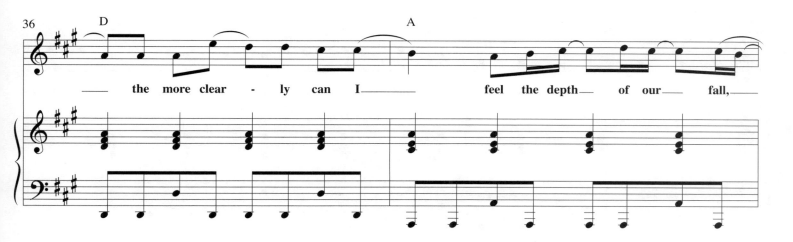

the most im - pos - si - ble thing:___ Your grand - ness in me,___

___ mak - ing me clean.___ Glo - ry, hal - le - lu - jah! Glo -

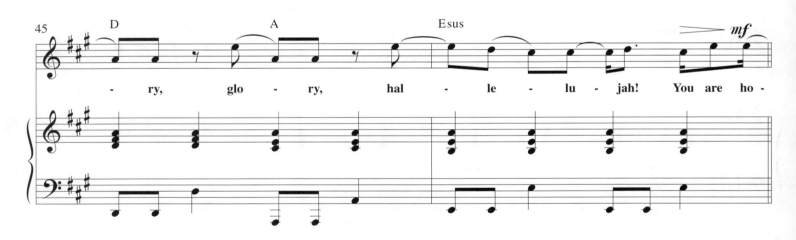

- ry, glo - ry, hal - le - lu - jah! You are ho -

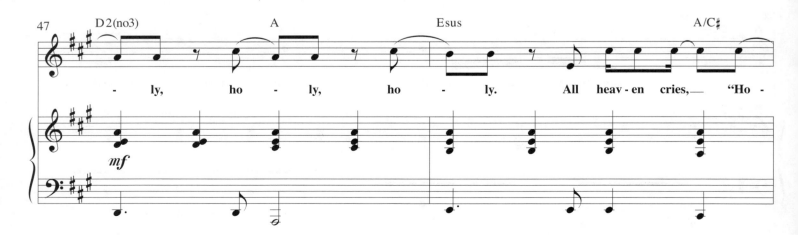

- ly, ho - ly, ho - ly. All heav - en cries,___ "Ho -

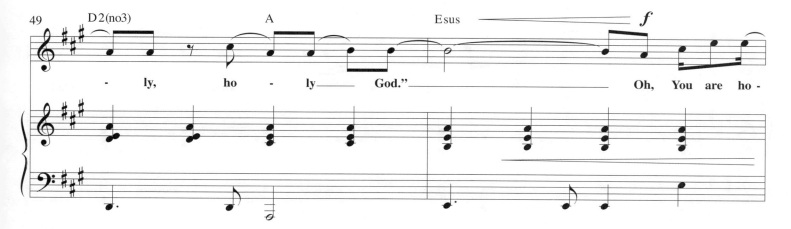

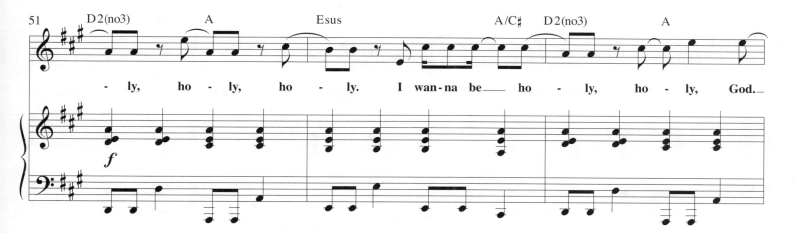

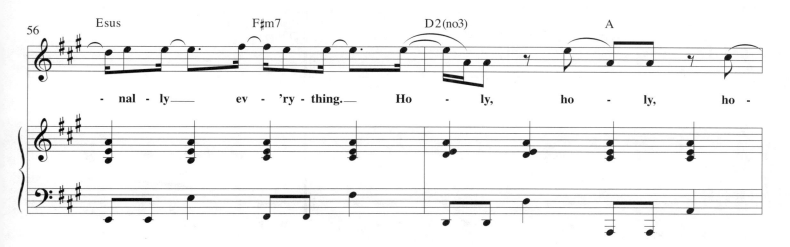

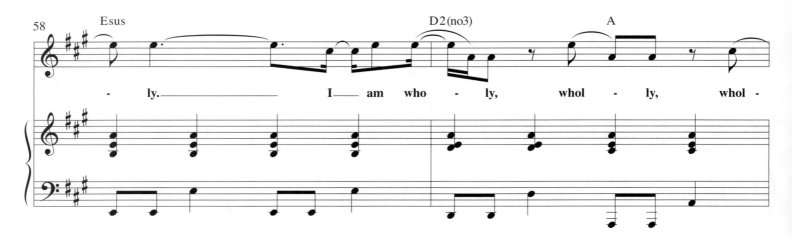

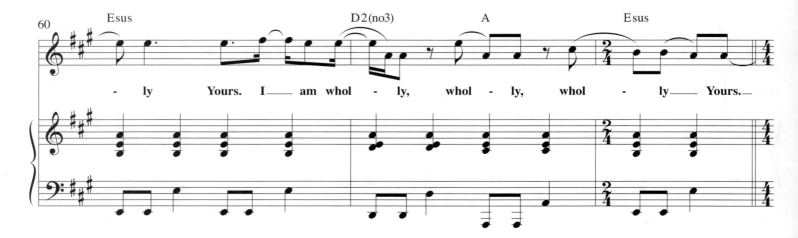

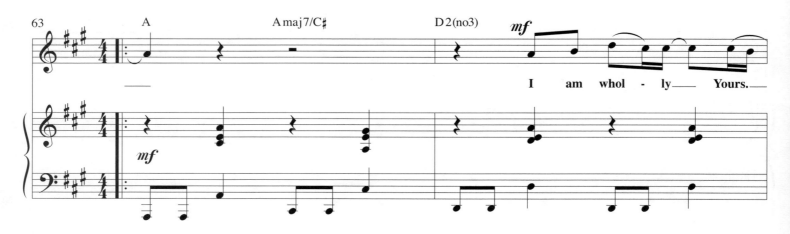

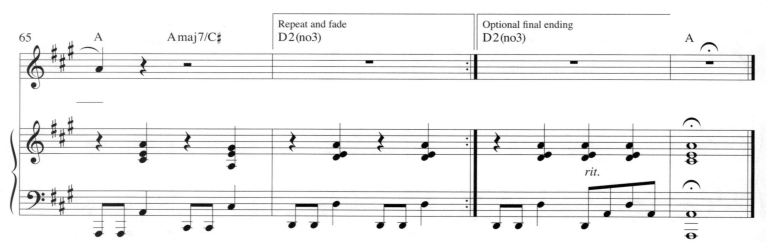

What If

Recorded by Nichole Nordeman

Words and Music by
NICHOLE NORDEMAN

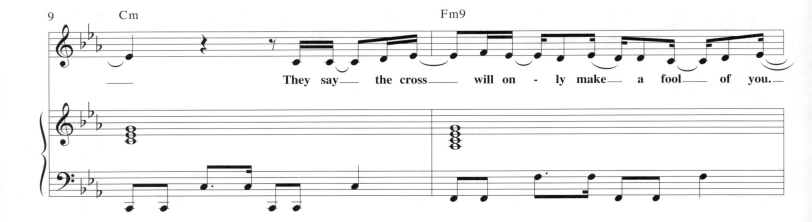

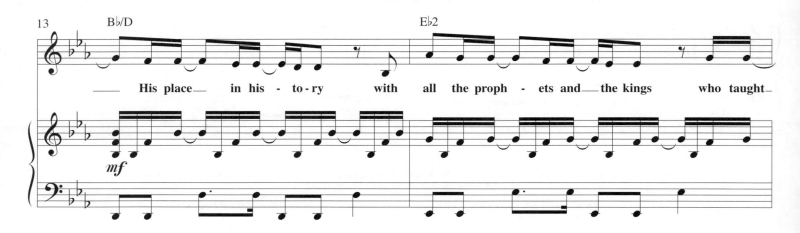

— us love— and came— in peace, but then the sto - ry— ends? What—

— then?— But what if you're wrong? What if there's—

— more?— What if— there's hope— you nev - er dreamed— of hop - ing for?—

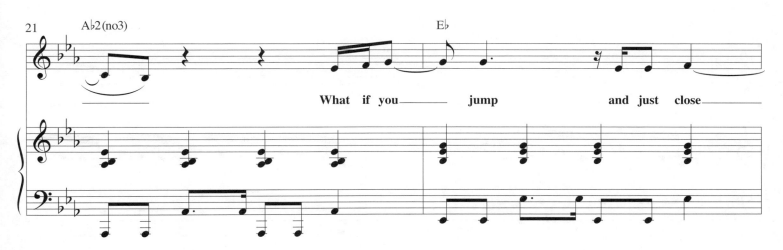

— What if you— jump and just close—

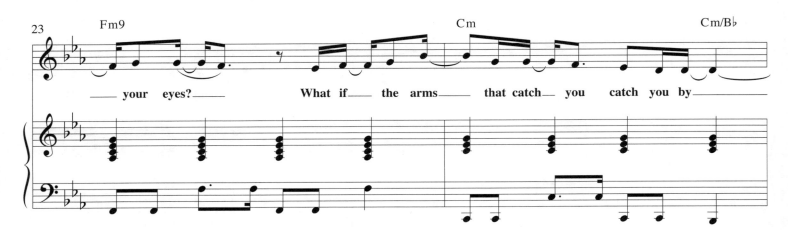

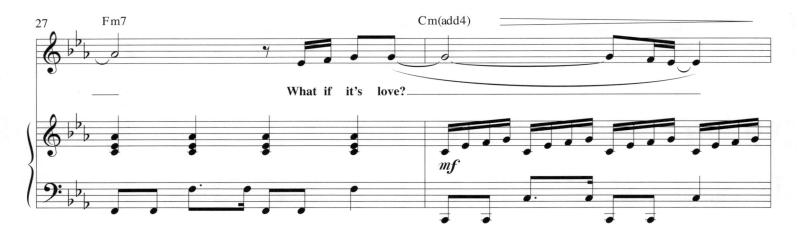

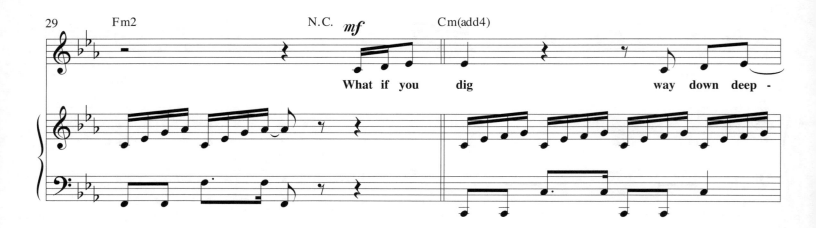

to poke the holes? What if the crown of thorns is no more than folk - lore

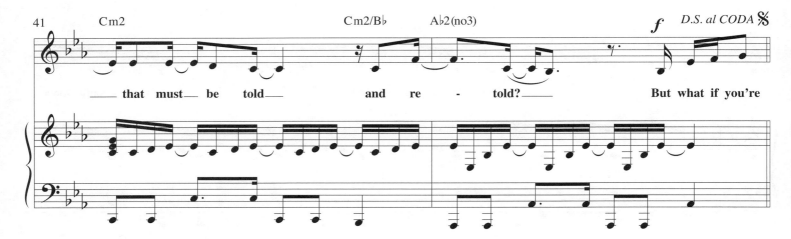

that must be told and re - told? But what if you're

What if it's love?

'Cause you've been run - ning as fast as you can.

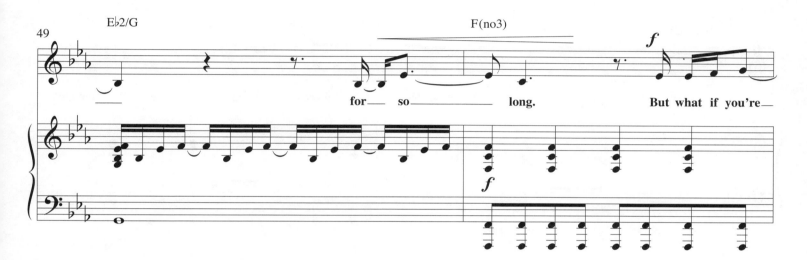

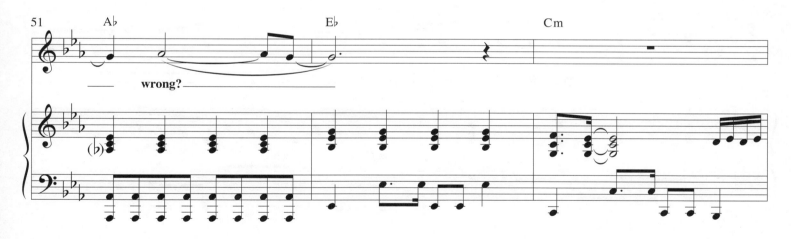

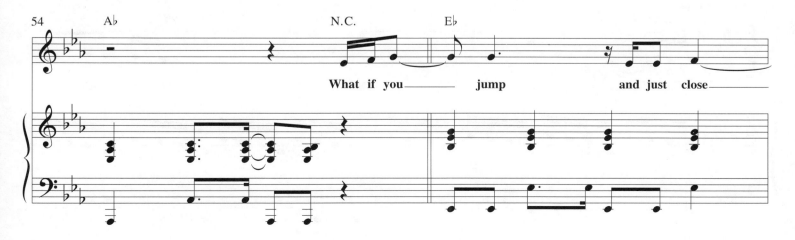

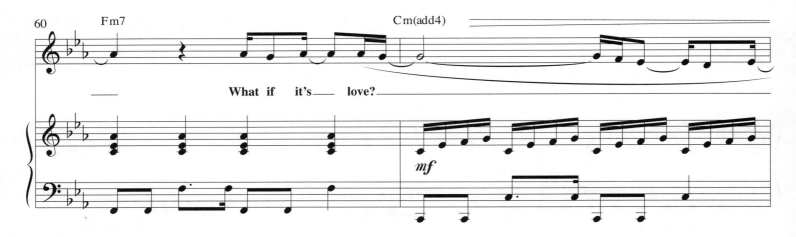

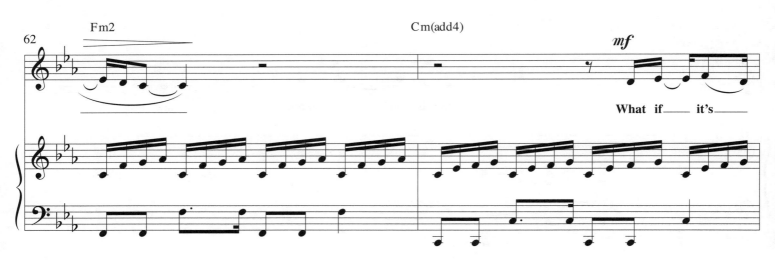

Welcome Home (You)

Recorded by Brian Littrell

Words and Music by
BRIAN LITTRELL and
DAN MUCKALA

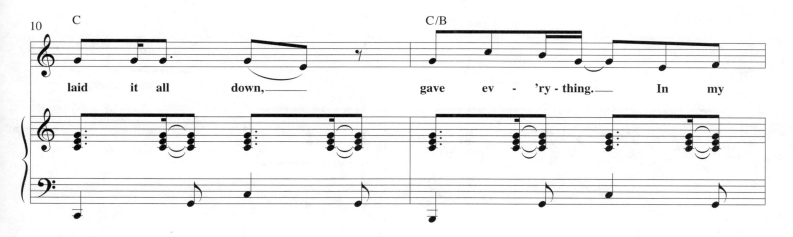

laid it all down,_____ gave ev - 'ry - thing._____ In my

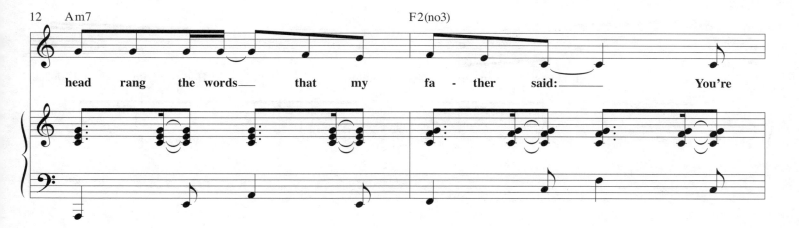

head rang the words_____ that my fa - ther said:_____ You're

nev - er far._____ I will be where you_____

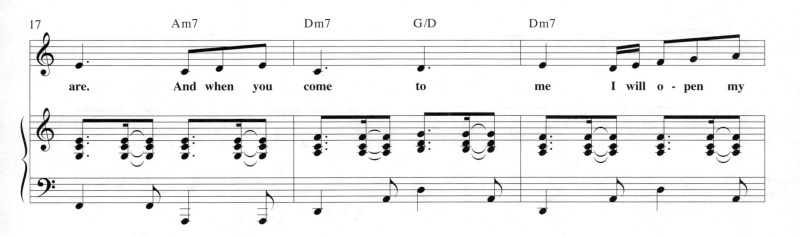

are. And when you come to me I will o - pen my

arms.

Wel - come home,

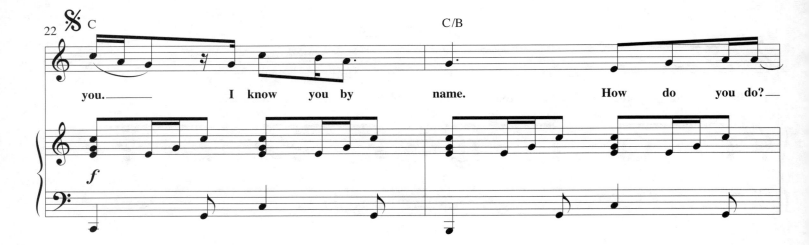

you._____ I know you by name. How do you do?_____

_____ I shine be - cause of you to - day. So come and sit down,_____

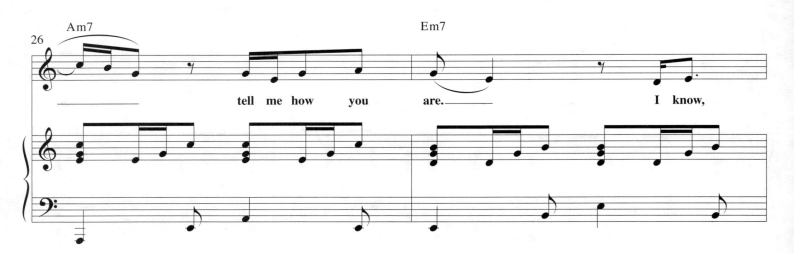

tell me how you are._____ I know,

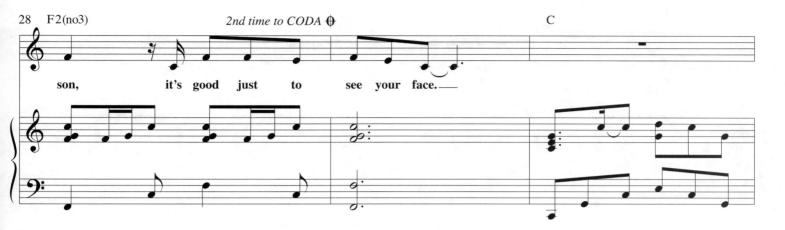

son, it's good just to see your face.___

When I

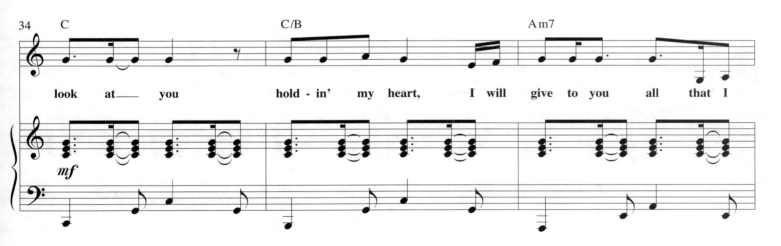

look at___ you hold-in' my heart, I will give to you all that I

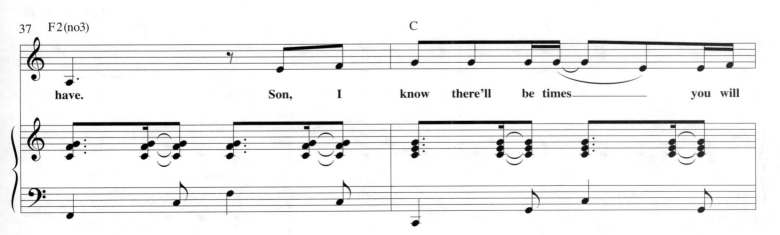

have. Son, I know there'll be times___ you will

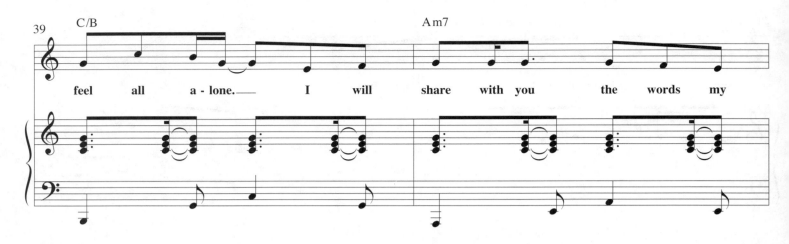

feel all a - lone.____ I will share with you the words my

Fa - ther said:____ You're nev - er far.____ I will be

where you_____ are. And when you come to

D.S. al CODA 𝄋

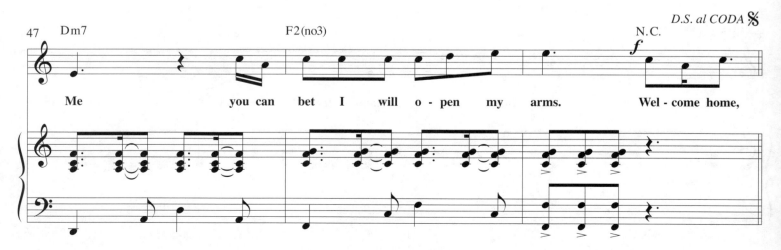

Me you can bet I will o - pen my arms. Wel - come home,

CODA

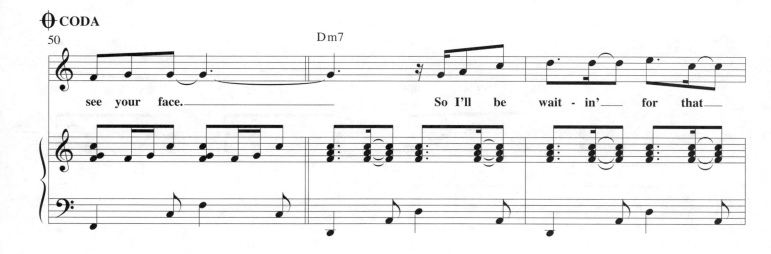

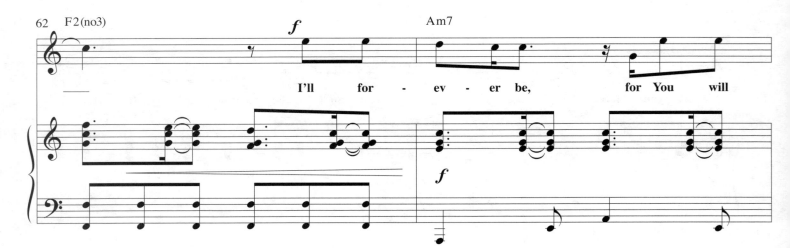

I'll for - ev - er be, for You will

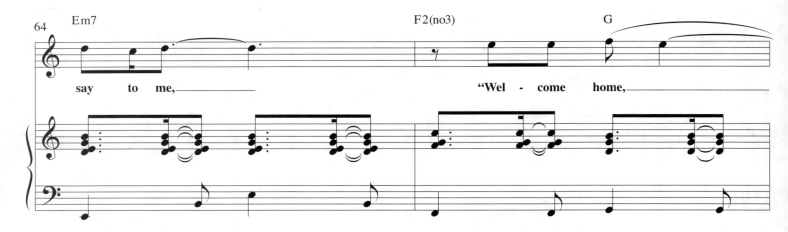

say to me,_____ "Wel - come home,_____

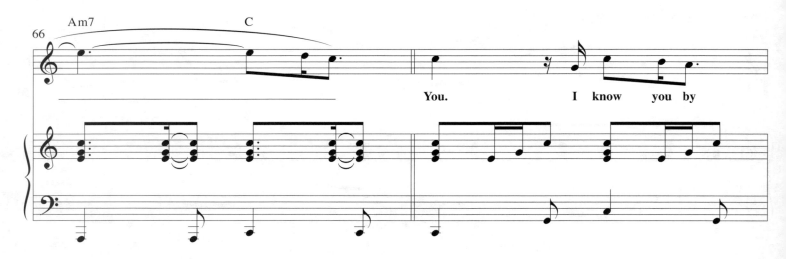

You. I know you by

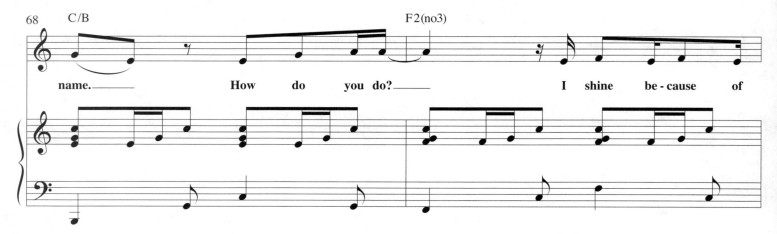

name._____ How do you do?_____ I shine be - cause of

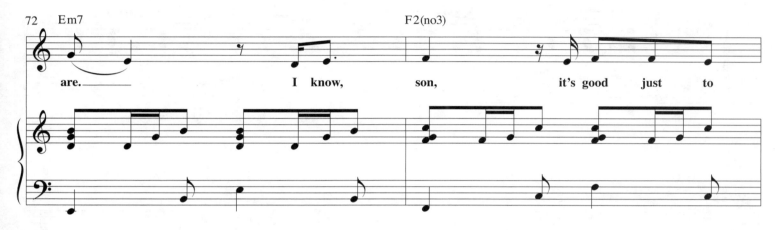

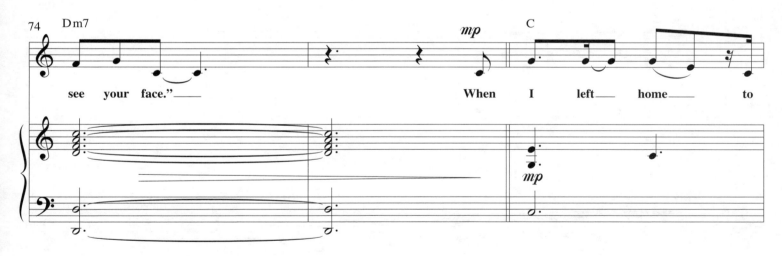

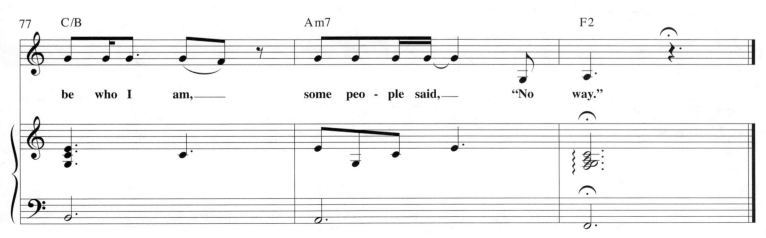

I AM

Recorded by Mark Schultz

**Words and Music by
MARK SCHULTZ**

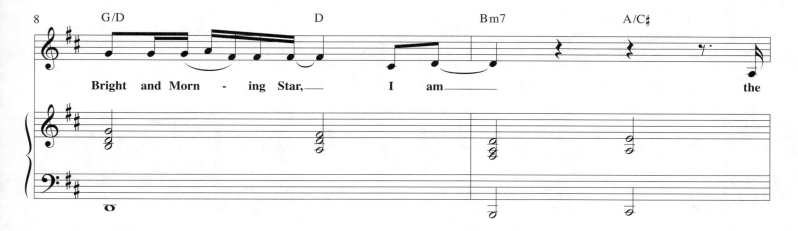

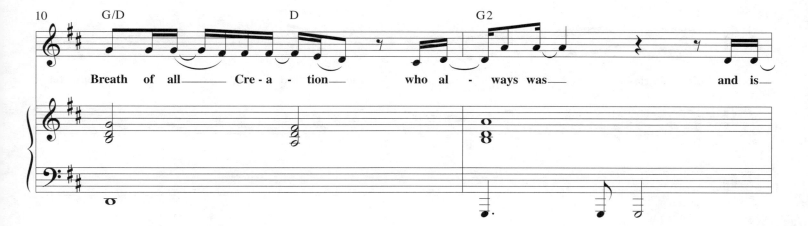

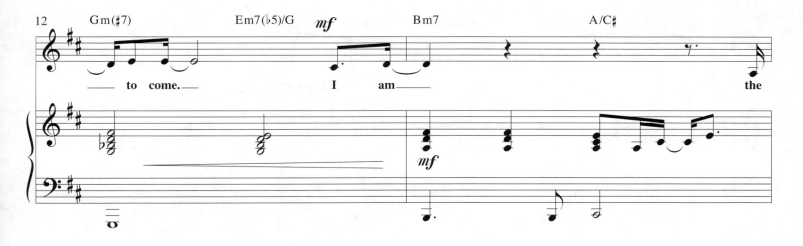

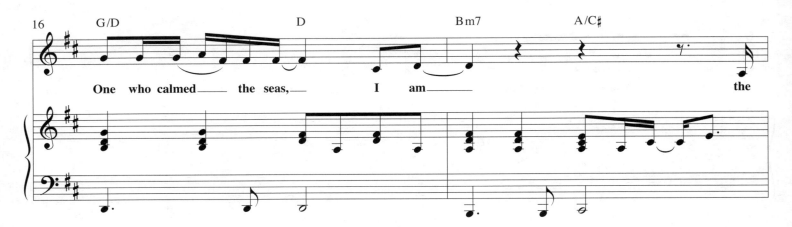

One who calmed the seas, I am the

Mir - a - cles and Won - ders. So come and see, oh, fol -

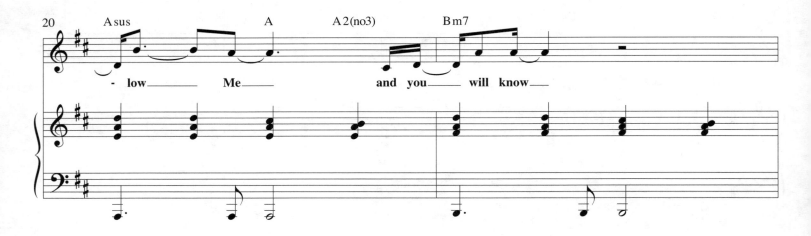

- low Me and you will know

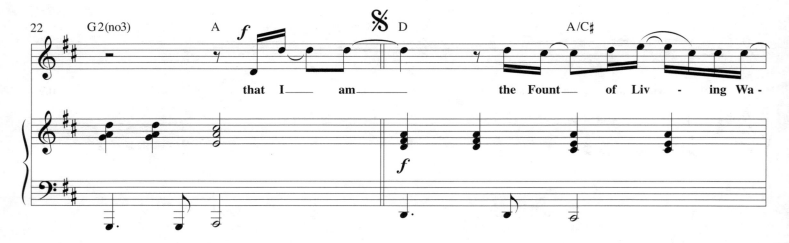

that I am the Fount of Liv - ing Wa -

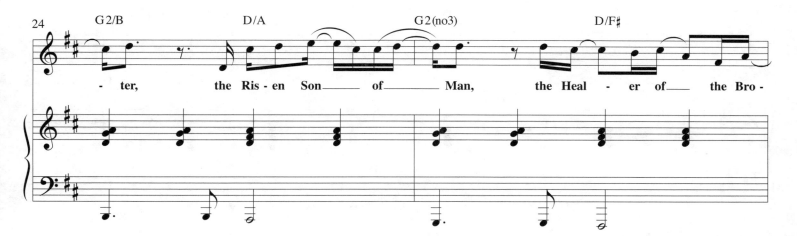

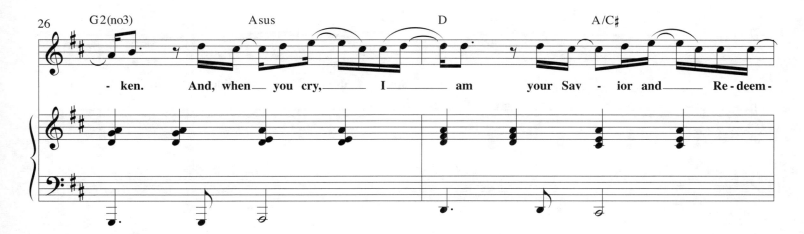

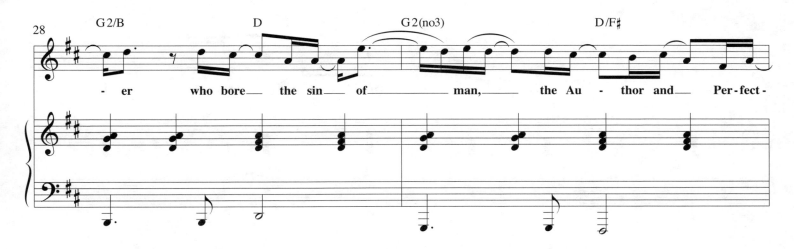

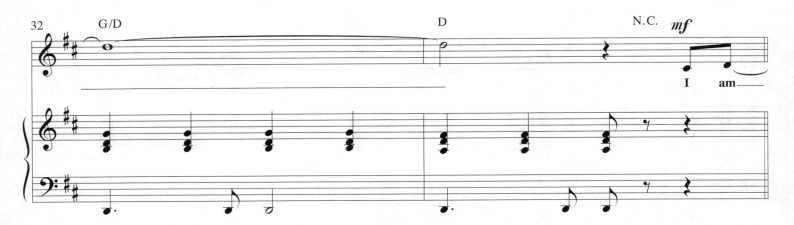

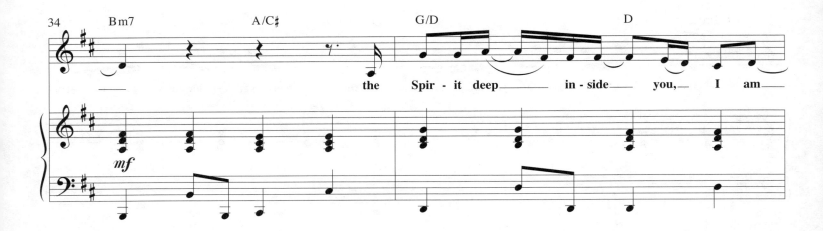

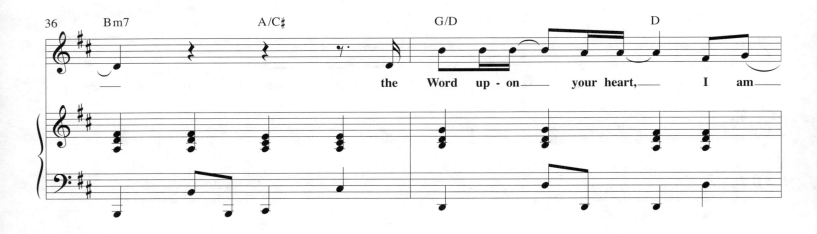

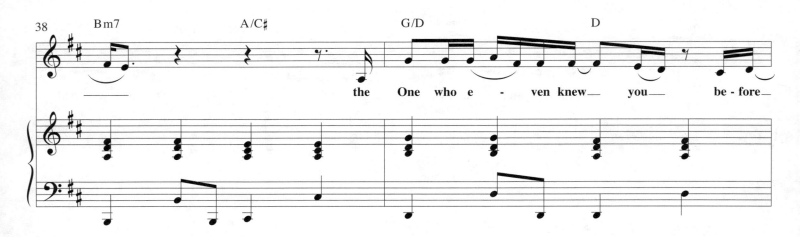

your birth, ___ be - fore ___ you ___ were. ___ I am

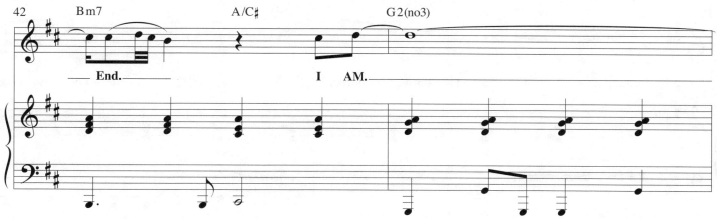

___ End. ___ I AM.

___ Yes, I ___ AM.

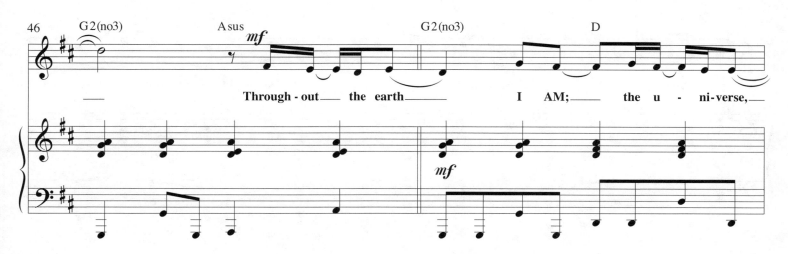

Through - out ___ the earth ___ I AM; ___ the u - ni-verse, ___

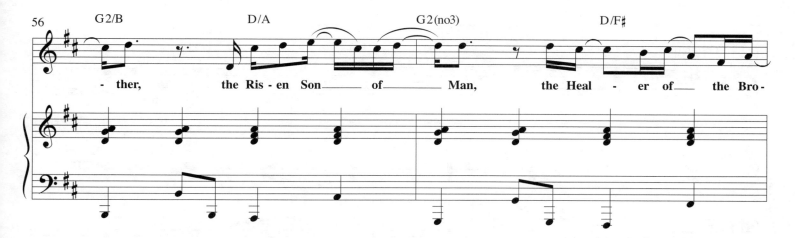

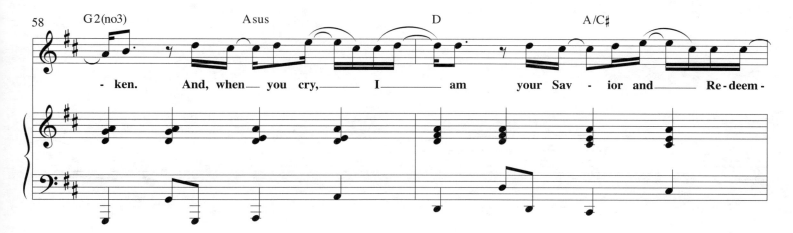

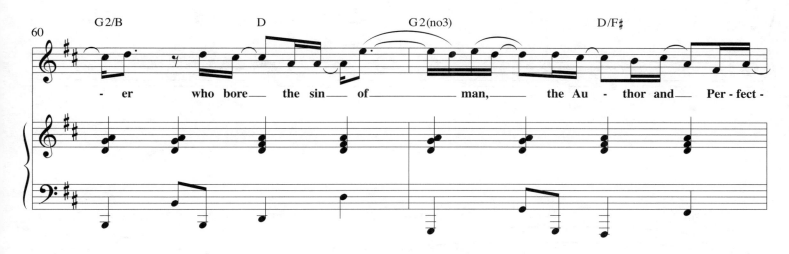

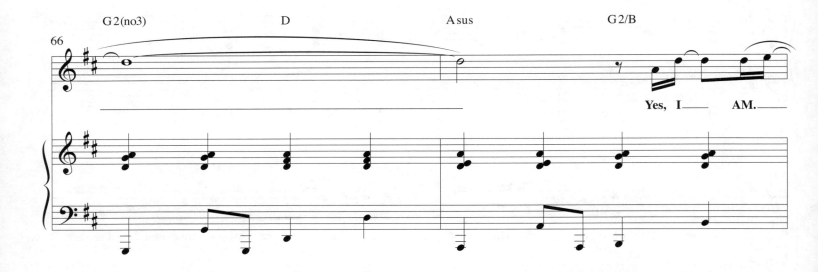

Here I Am

Recorded by Michael W. Smith

**Words and Music by
MICHAEL W. SMITH
and MARTIN SMITH**

Steady four ♩ = 100

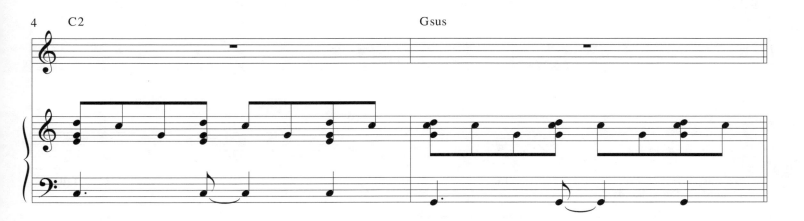

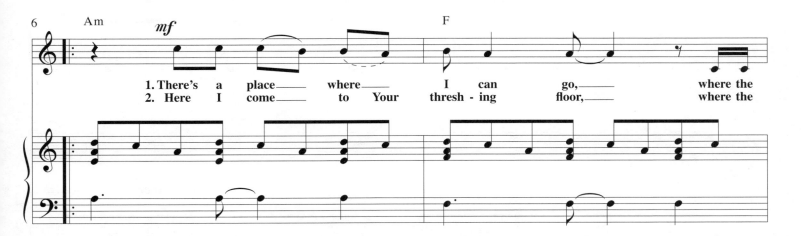

1. There's a place where I can go, where the
2. Here I come to Your thresh-ing floor, where the

an - gels   hear___ me   pray.
an - gels   fear___ to   tread.___

I   want   to   change;___   Yes,   I   need Your   touch.___   I'm
I'm   wait - ing   here___   Yes,   for   the   King   of   love,___   and to

wait - ing   here___   for   You.___   And   I   fall,
hold   the   hands___   that   bled.___

at   Your   feet.___

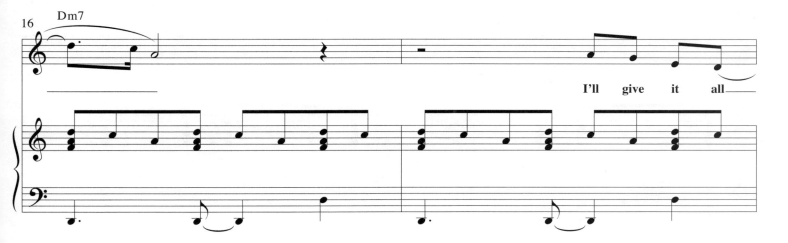

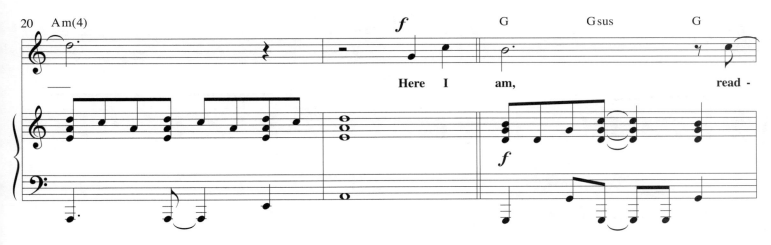

for the Son.

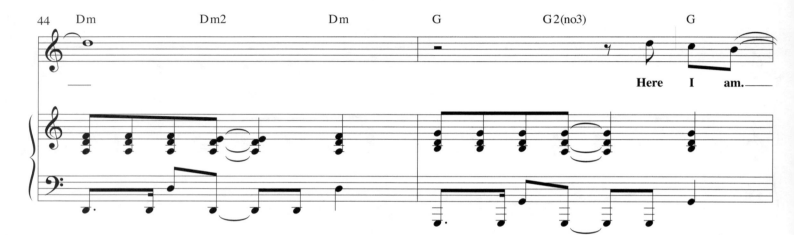

Here I am.

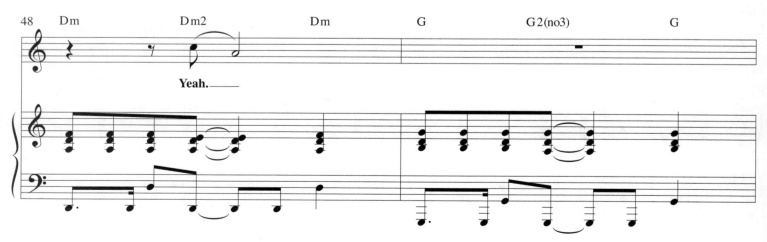

Yeah.

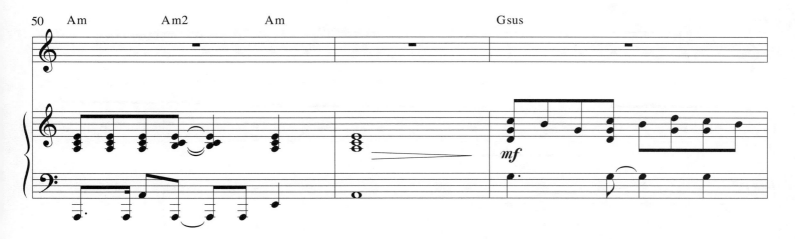

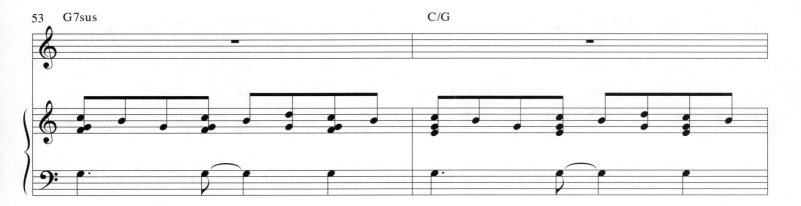

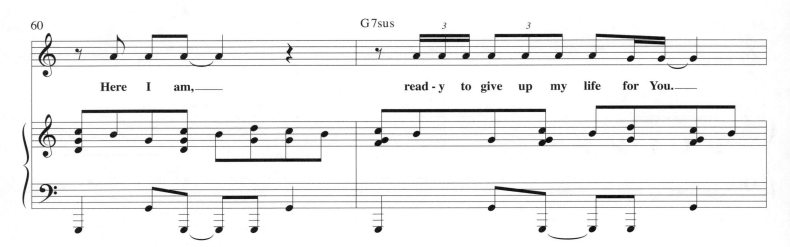

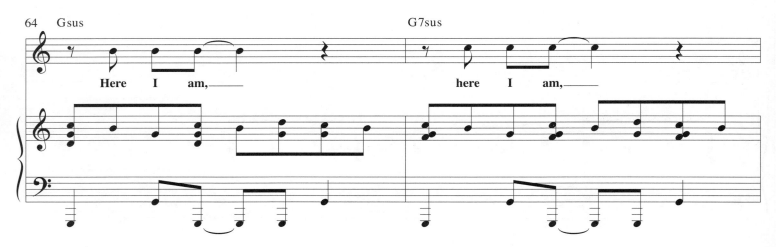

I Am Free

Recorded by The Newsboys

**Words and Music by
JOE EGAN and
PETE FURLER**

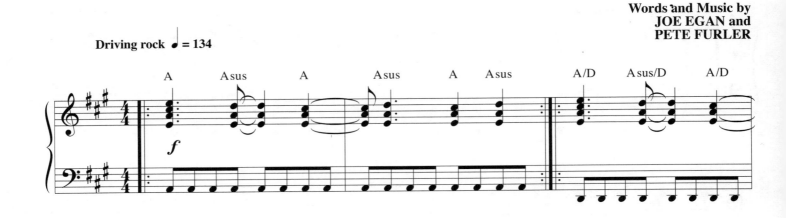

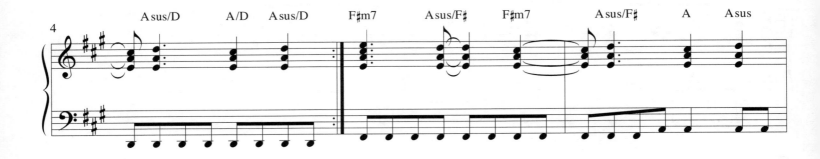

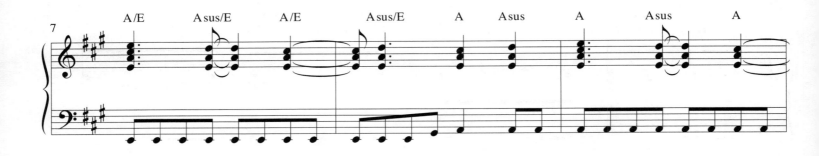

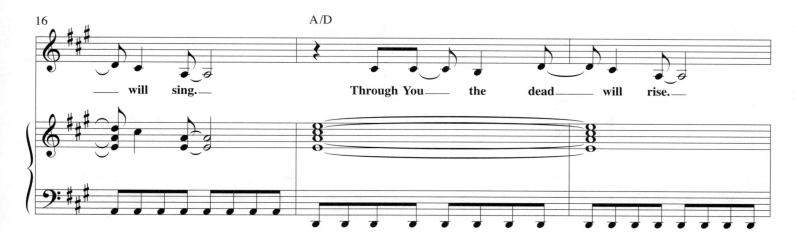

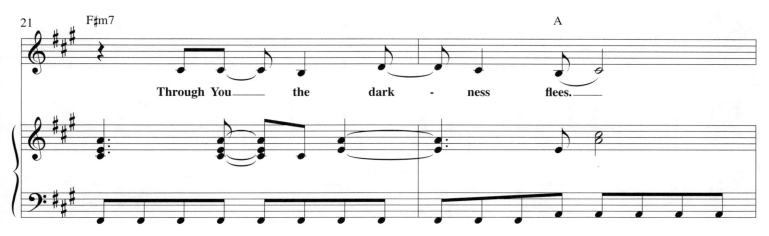

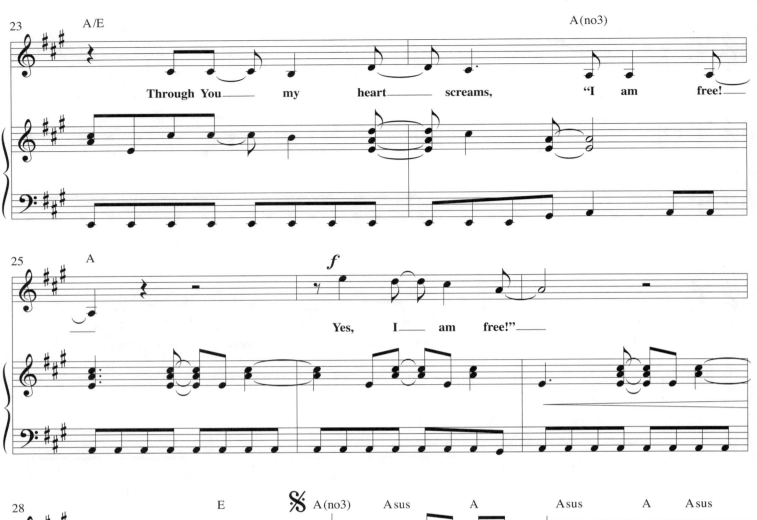

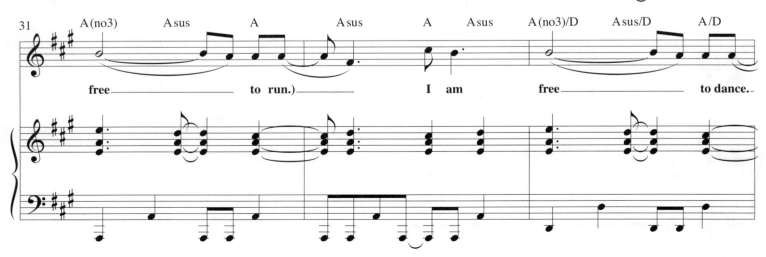

120

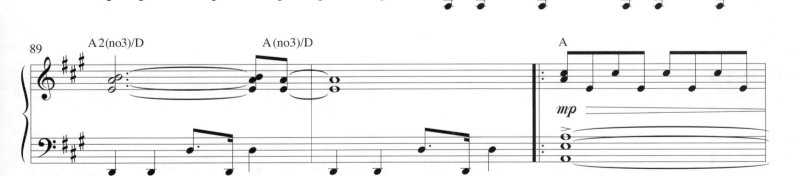

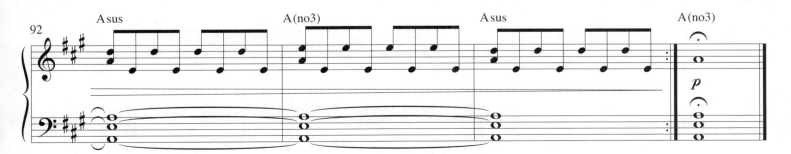

Without You

Recorded by Big Daddy Weave

Words and Music by
MICHAEL WEAVER, JAY WEAVER
and JEREMY REDMON

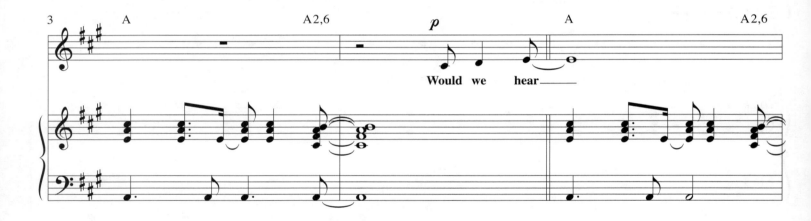

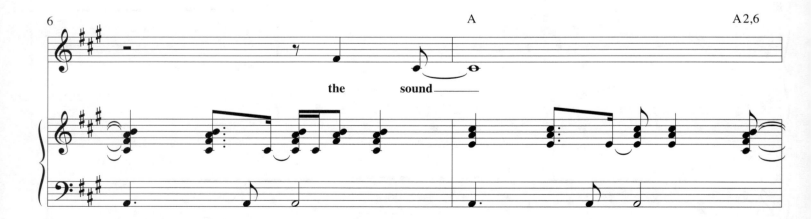

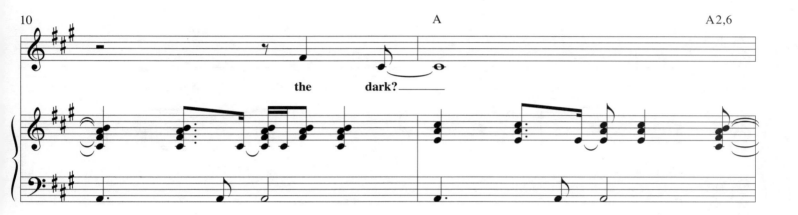

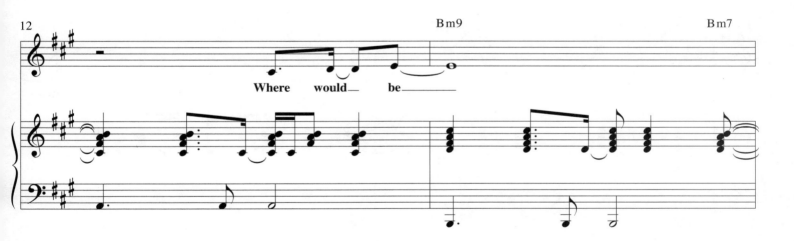

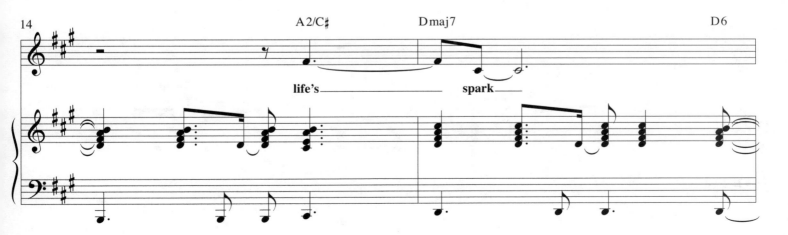

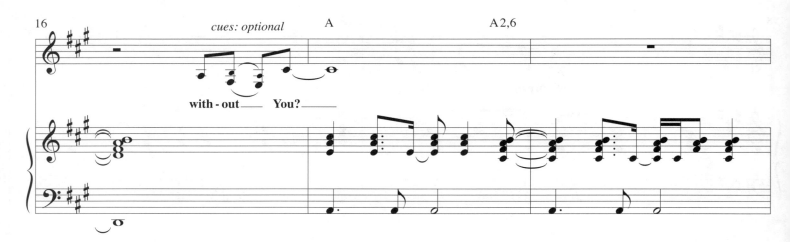

with - out____ You?____

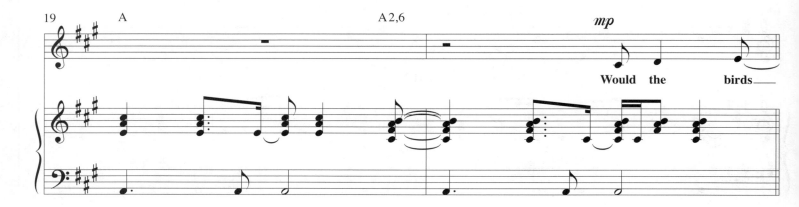

Would the birds____

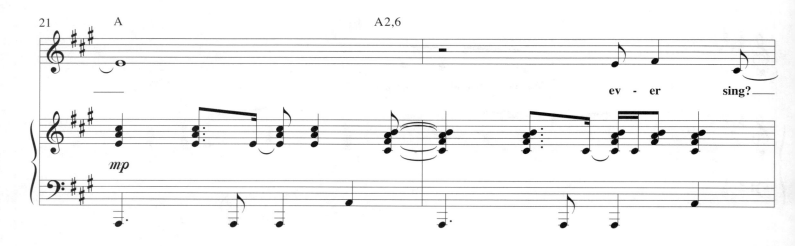

____ ev - er sing?____

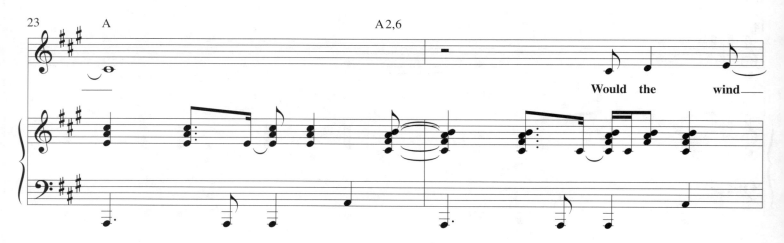

Would the wind____

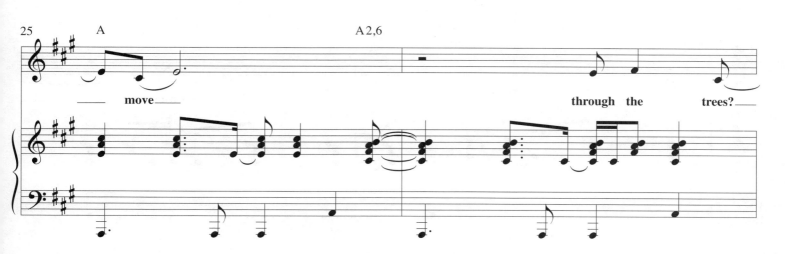

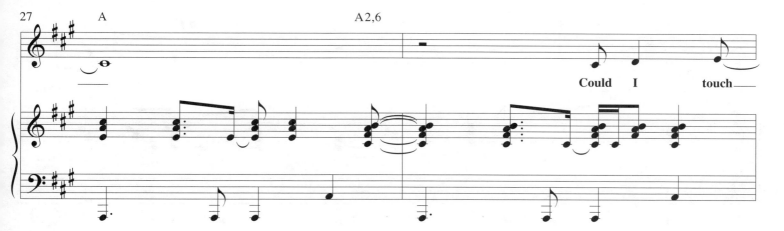

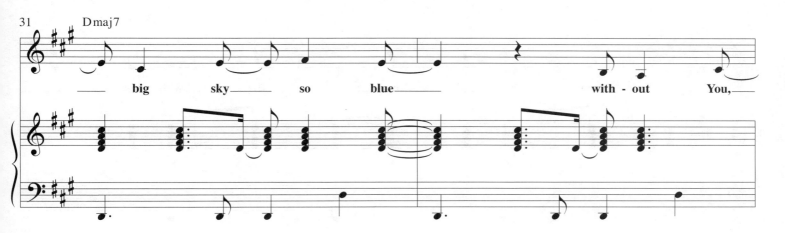

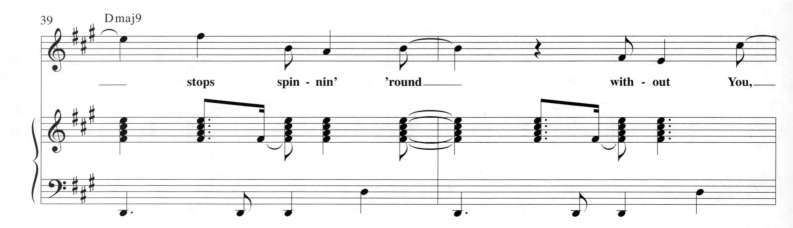

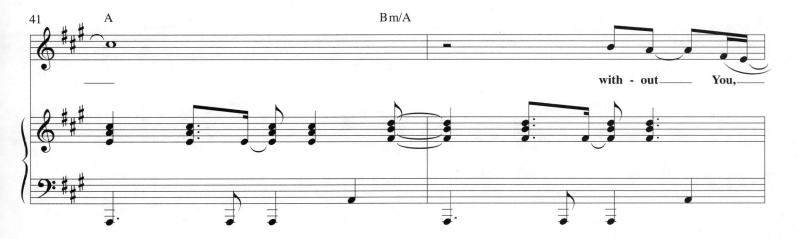

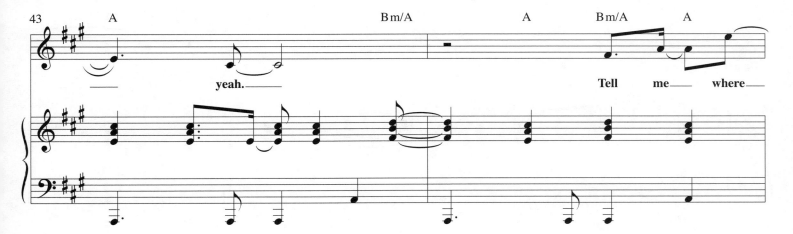

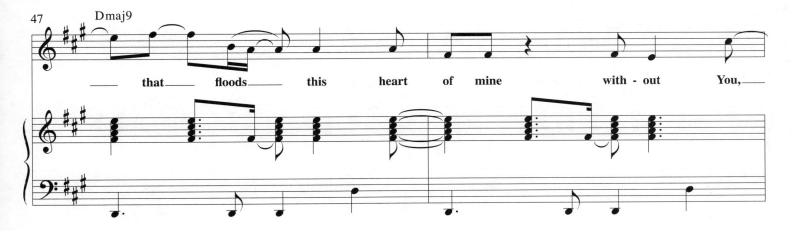

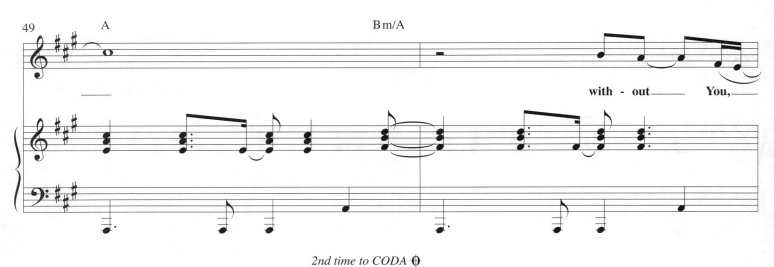

2nd time to CODA ⊕

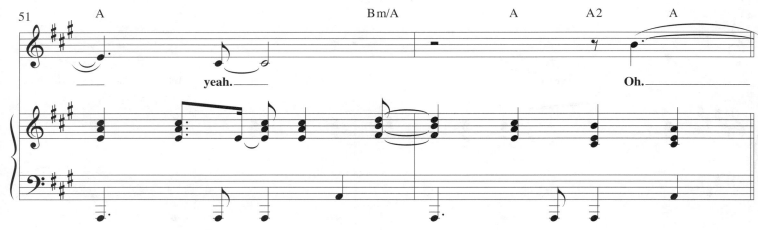

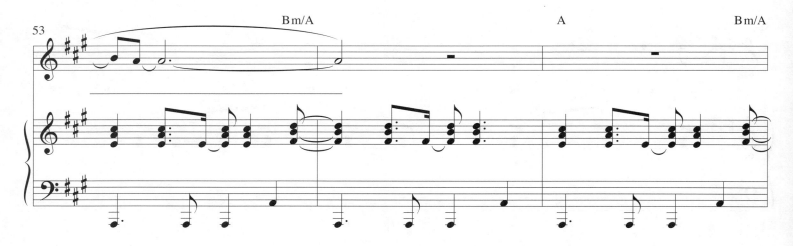

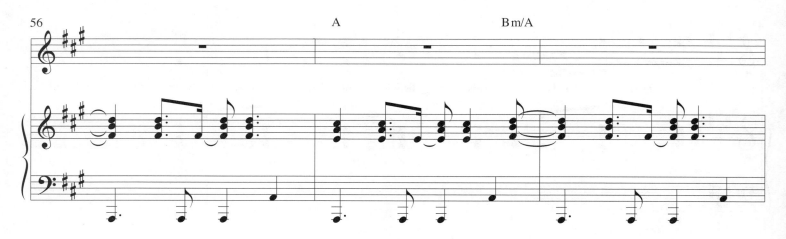

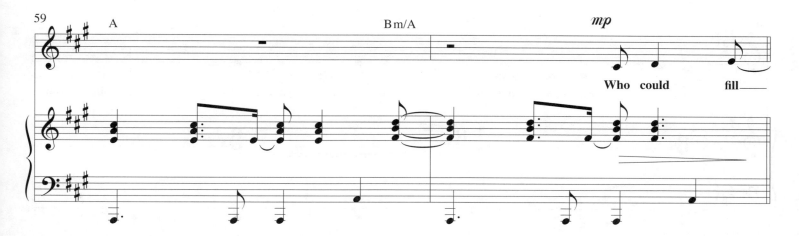

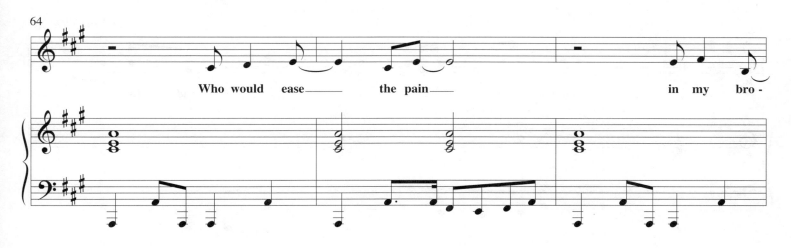

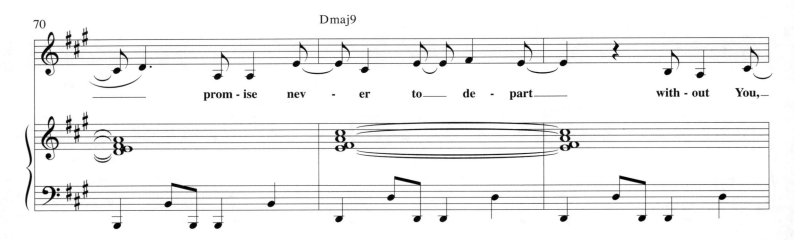

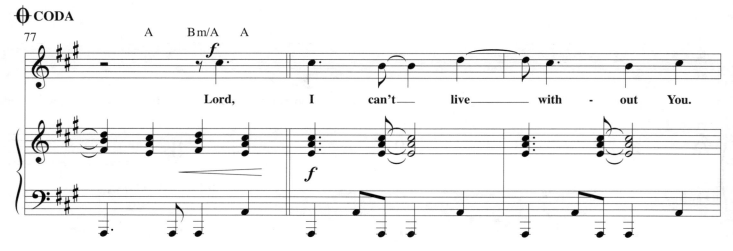

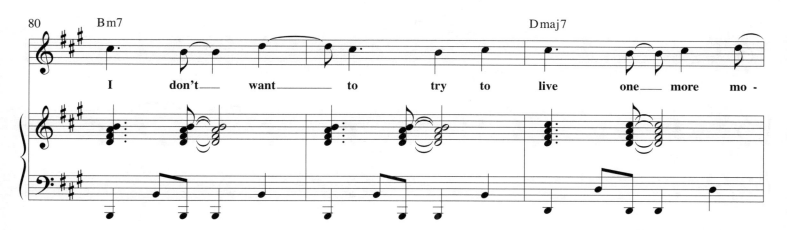

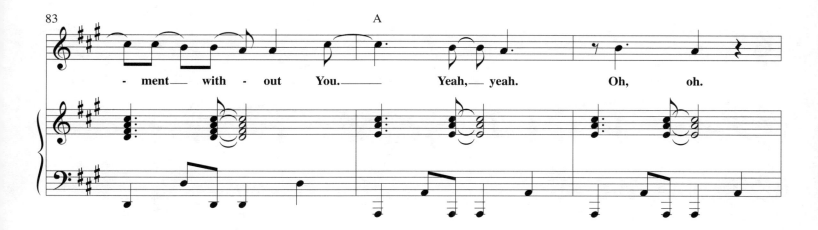

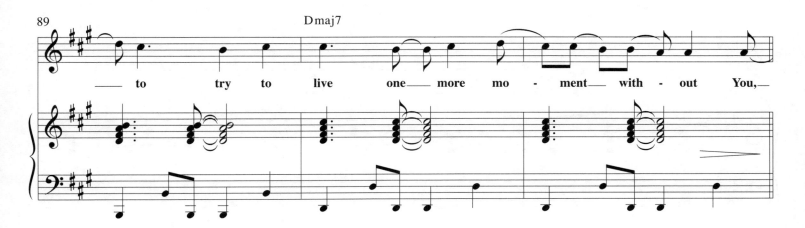

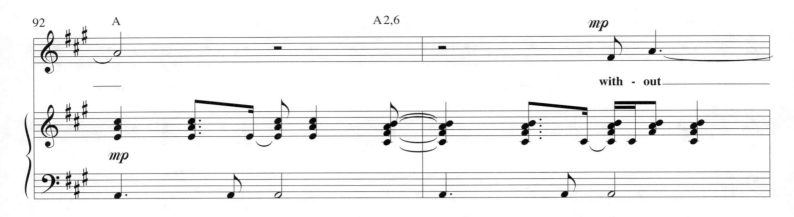

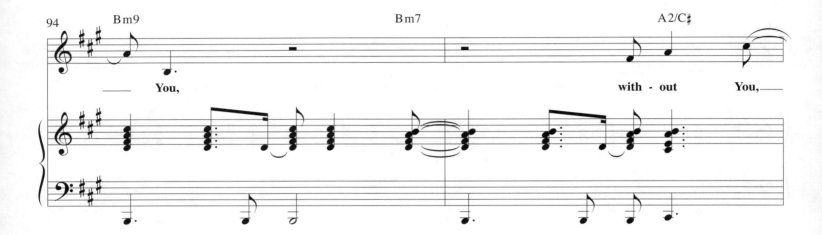

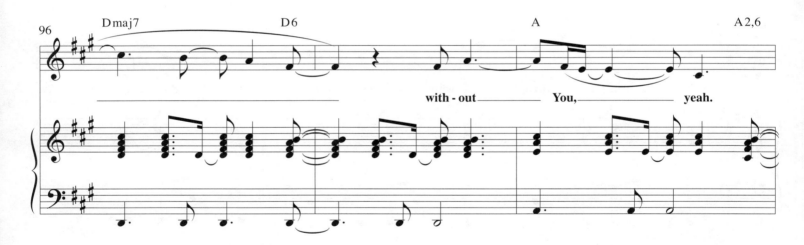

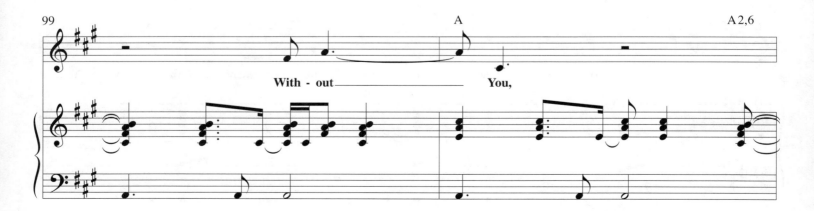

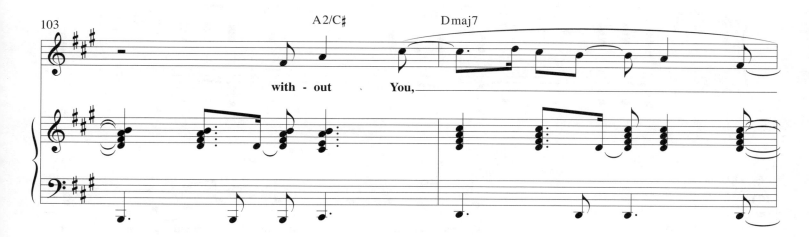

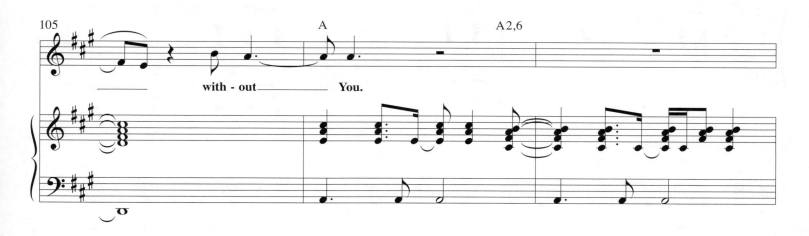

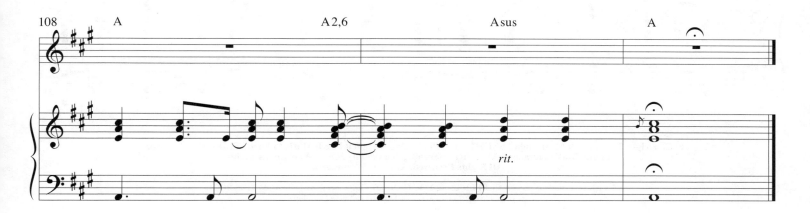

Happy

Recorded by Ayiesha Woods

Words and Music by
AYIESHA WOODS, JAMIE MOORE
and DAVID MULLEN

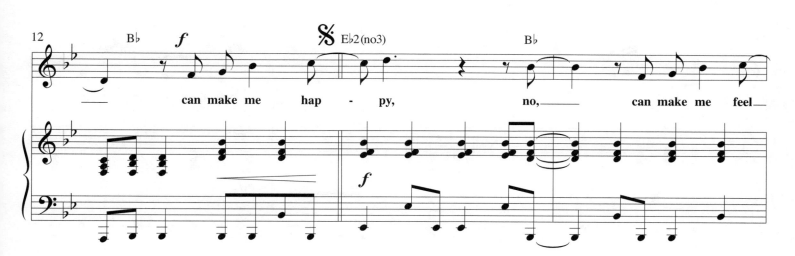

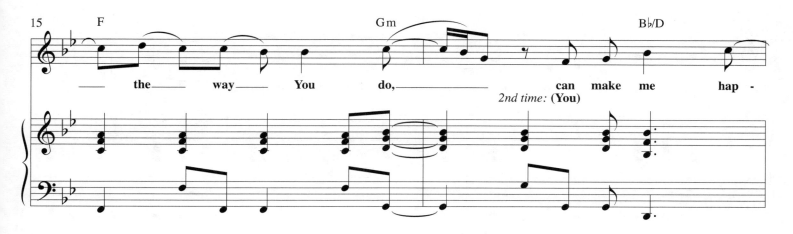

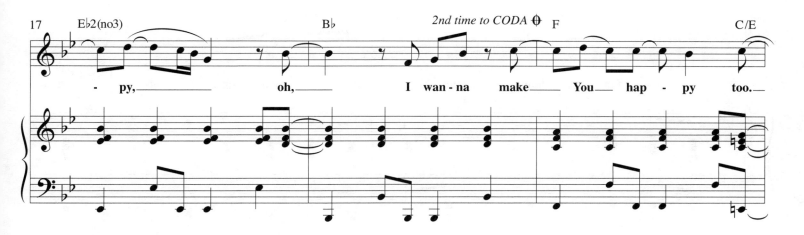

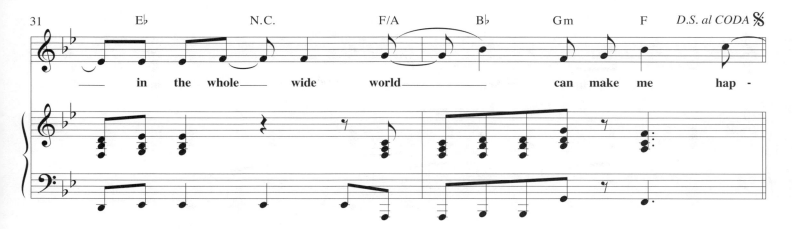

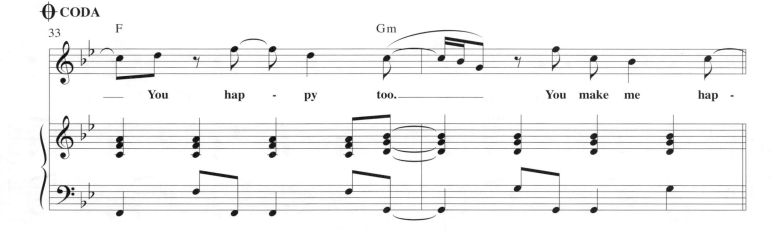

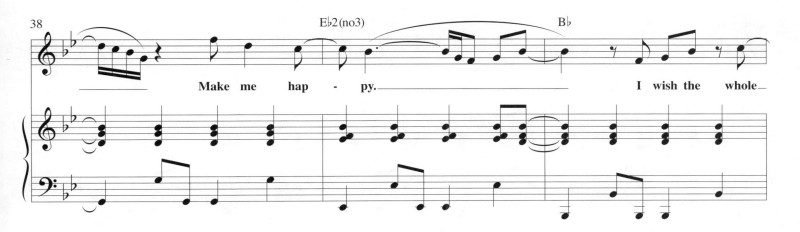

world___ knew___ You too.___ Sing - ing: La___

___ la la___ la la___ la, La la la___ la la la la,

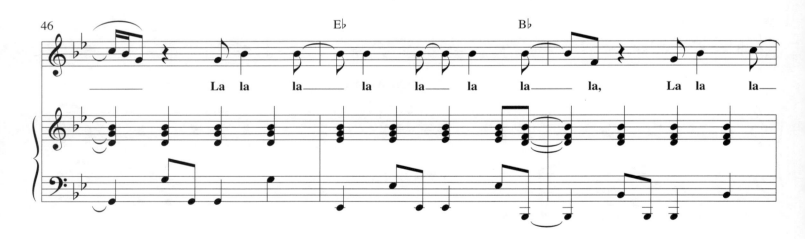

___ La la la___ la la___ la la___ la, La la la___

___ la la la la.___ No, I can -

52

Eb .... Bb .... F

- not count the ways You have made my life so blessed.

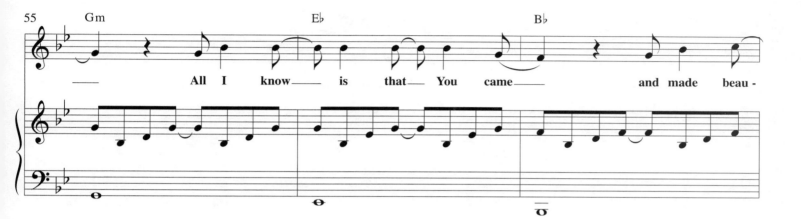

55

Gm .... Eb .... Bb

All I know is that You came and made beau -

58

F .... Gm .... Eb

- ty of my mess. Said, I can - not count the ways

61

Bb .... F .... Gm

that You have made my life so blessed. All I know

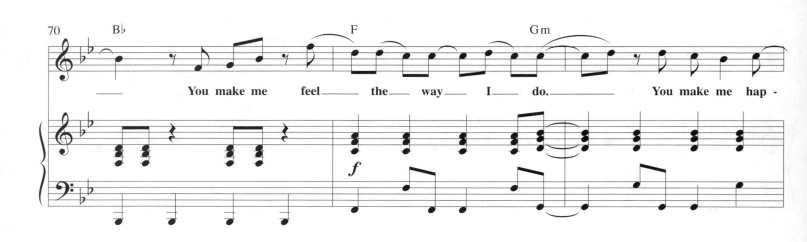

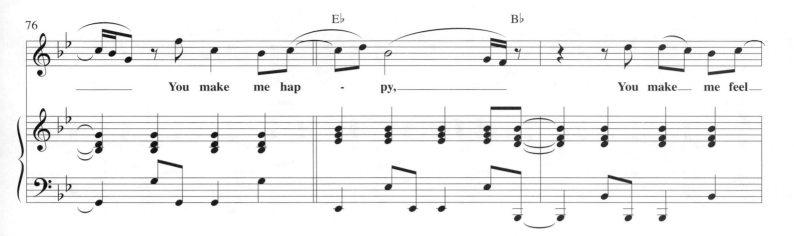

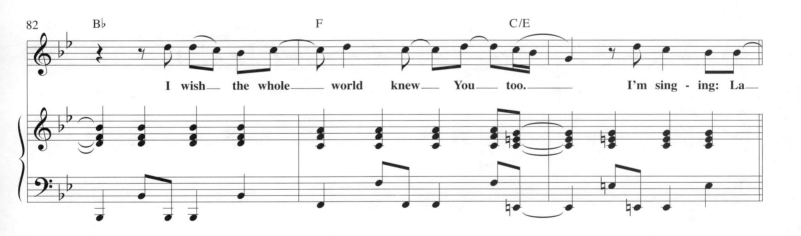

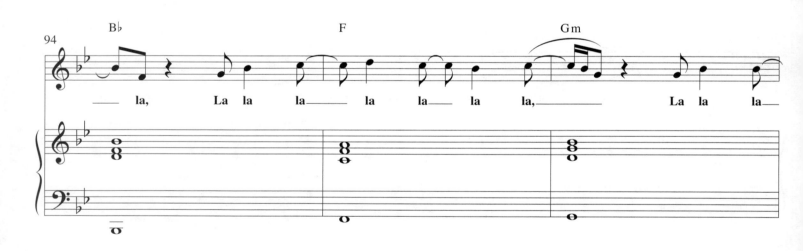

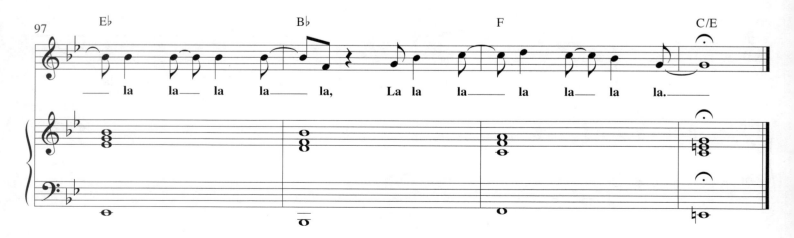

Let Go

Recorded by BarlowGirl

Words and Music by
BARLOWGIRL

Driving rock beat ♩ = 128

1. Yeah, I ___ trust in You. ___
2. What is this ___ doubt in me ___

I re-mem-ber times ___ You led ___ me.
con-vinc-ing me to fear ___ the un - known?

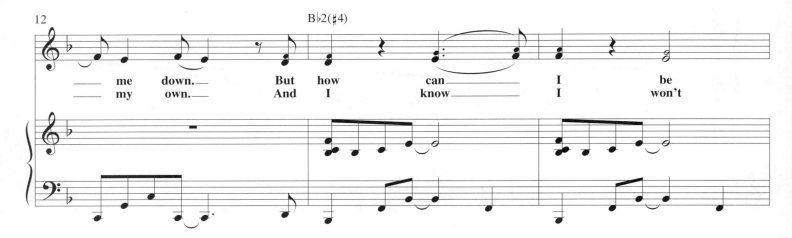

Burn for You

Recorded by tobyMac

Words and Music by
TOBY McKEEHAN, ROBERT MARVIN
and JASIAH BELL

Moderate rock ♩ = 112

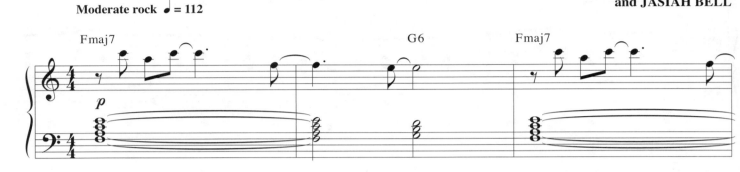

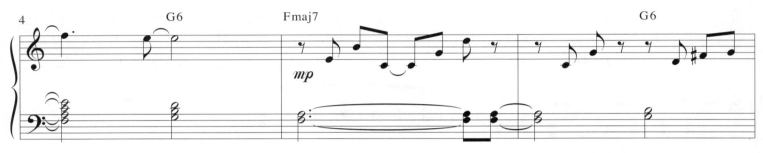

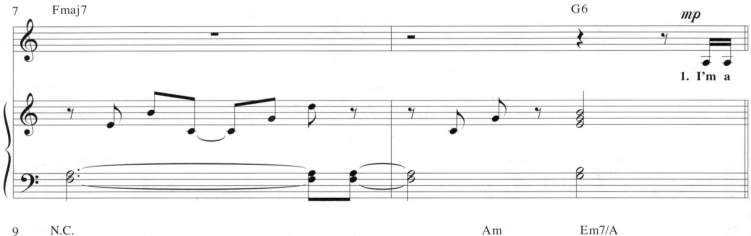

brand new man, I'm a con-scious man, I'm a man who's burn-in' for You. The mis-

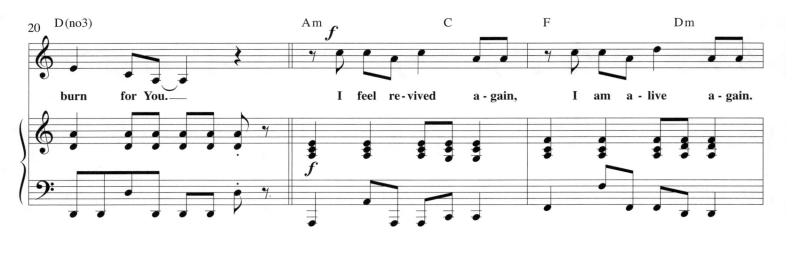

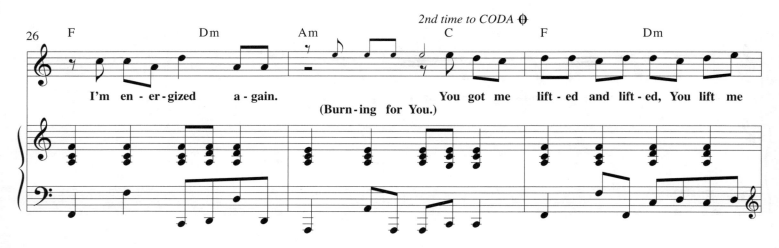

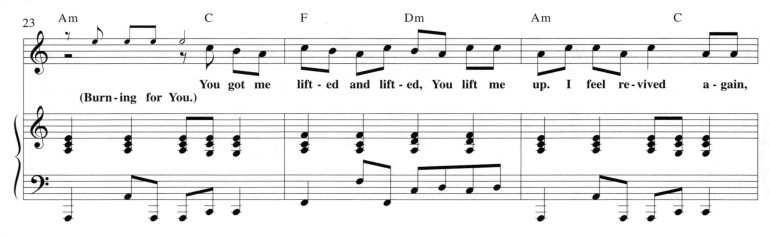

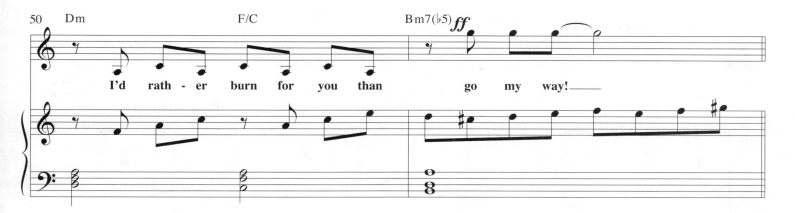

I'd rath - er burn for you than go my way!___

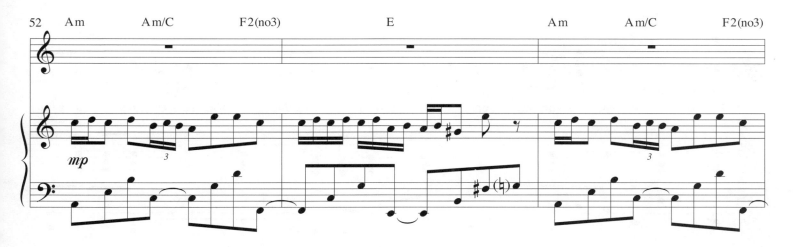

I want the world to know I burn for You.___

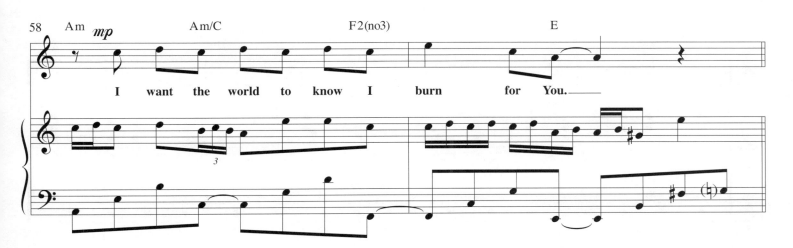

Who I Am Hates Who I've Been

Recorded by Relient K

Words and Music by
MATT THIESSEN

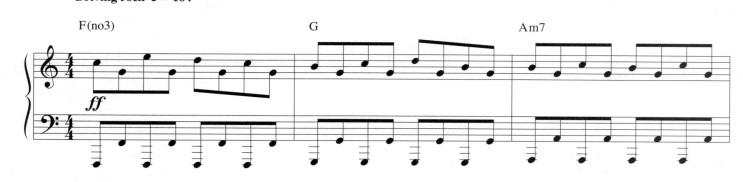

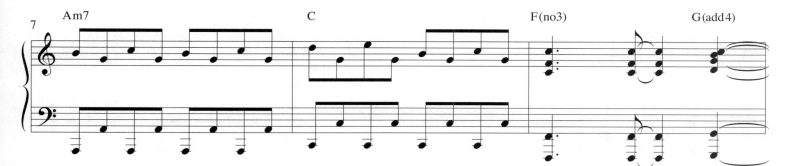

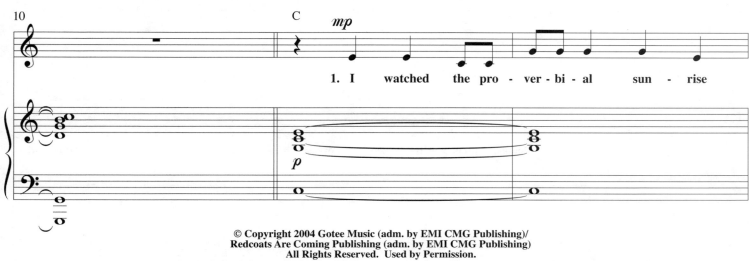

1. I watched the pro - ver - bi - al sun - rise

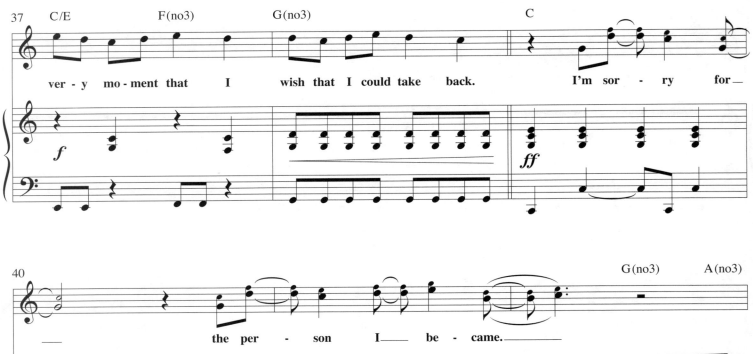

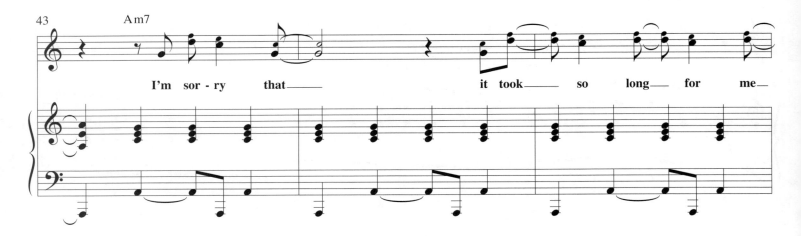

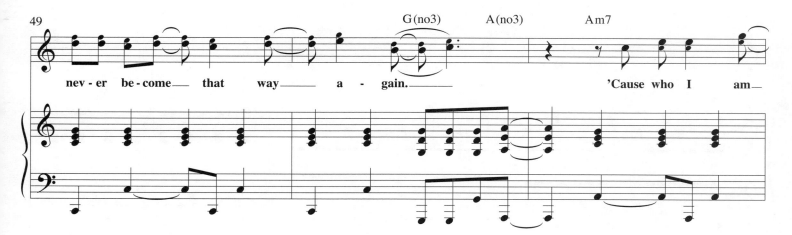

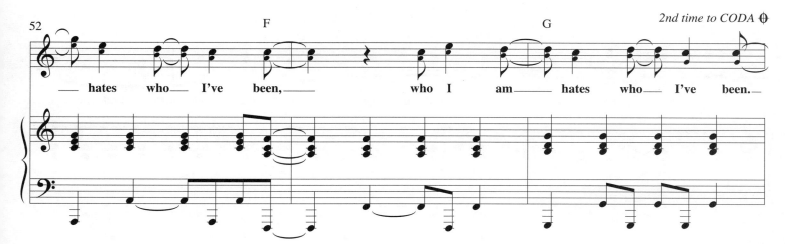

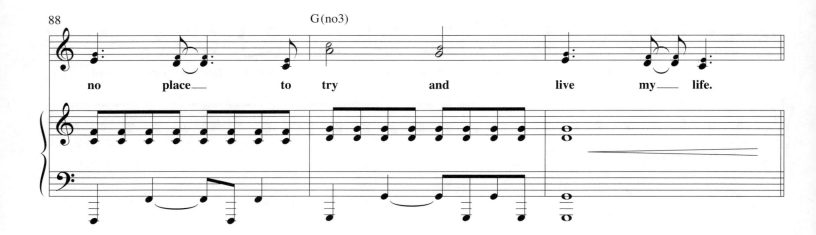

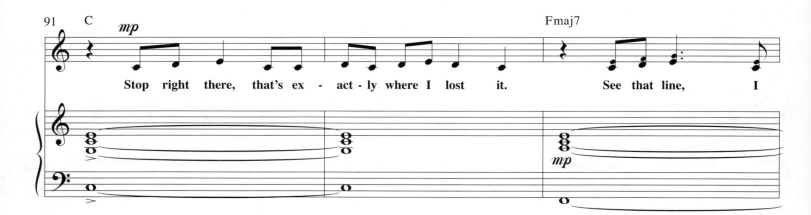

D.S. al CODA 𝄋

97 G(add 4)

rit.

ver - y mo - ment that I wished——— that I could take back.

CODA

99 C/E   *f*   F(no3)   C(no3) *ff*

——— Who I am hates who—— I've been,——— and who I am will take the

102 G#dim   Am   *f*   F

sec - ond chance You gave me.   Who I am——— hates who—— I've been,—

105 C   *ff* G   C

——— 'cause who I've been   on - ly ev - er made me——— so sor - ry for—

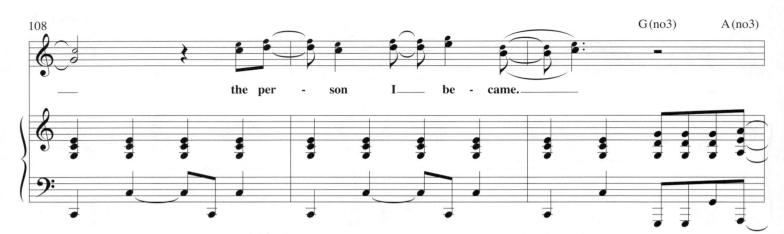

the per - son I____ be - came.____

So sor - ry that____ it took____ so long____ for me

____ to change.____ I'm read - y to____ try and

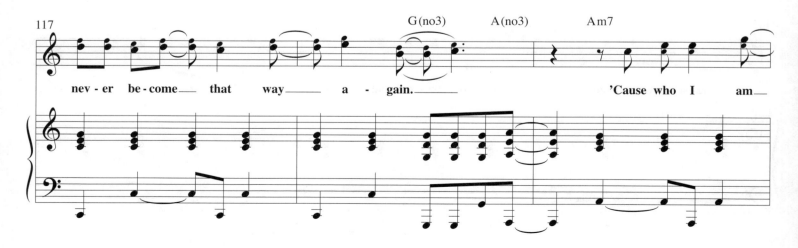

nev - er be - come____ that way____ a - gain.____ 'Cause who I am____

We Live

Recorded by Superchic[k]

**Words and Music by
MAX HSU, MATT DALLY, DAVE GHAZARIAN,
TRICIA BROCK and MELISSA BROCK**

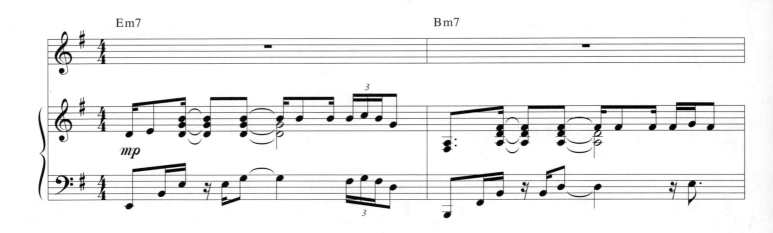

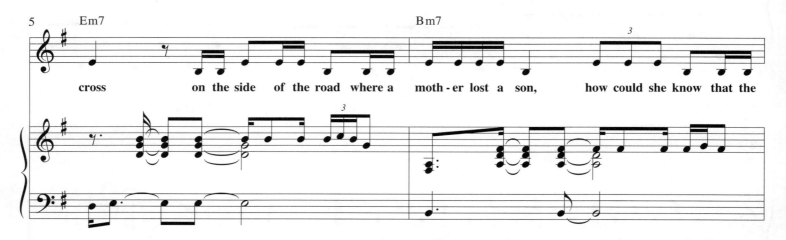

cross   on the side   of the road   where a   moth-er lost a son,   how could she know that the

morn-ing he left would be their last time. She'd trade with him for a lit-tle more time so

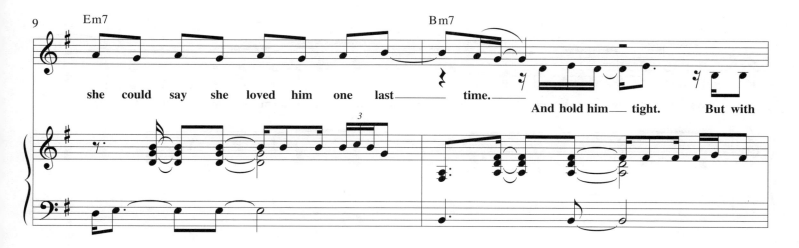

she could say she loved him one last time. And hold him tight. But with

life we nev-er know when we're com-ing up to the end of the road.

So what do we do then, with trag-e-dy a-round the bend?

168

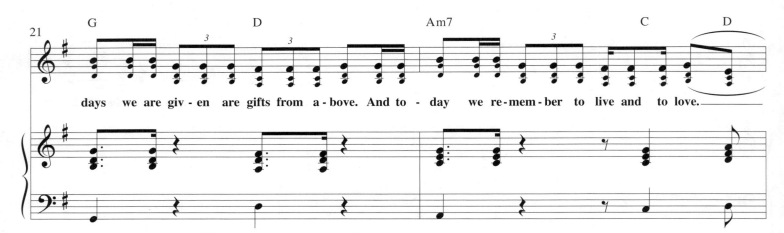

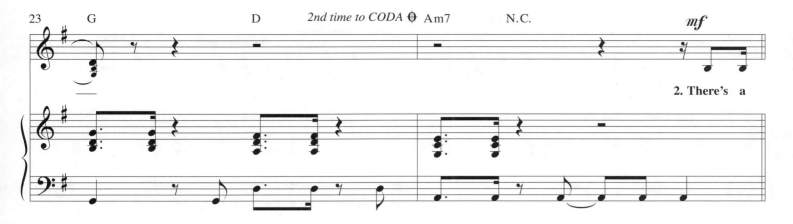

2nd time to CODA

2. There's a

man   who waits for the tests   to   see if the can - cer has   spread yet.   And

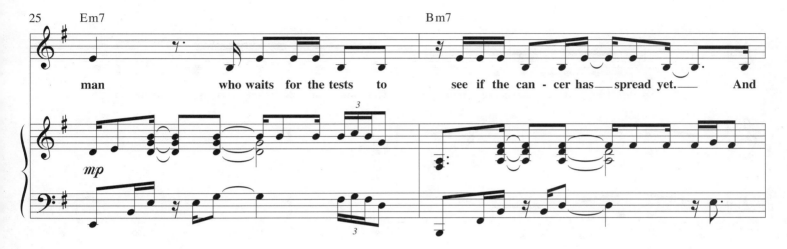

now   he asks,   "So why   did I   wait   to live   'til it was   time   to die?   If

I could have   the time   back,   how I'd   live."   Life is such   a gift.

So how does the sto-ry end?—— Well, this is your sto-ry and it all de-pends.——

D.S. al CODA

So don't let it—— be-come true. Get out and do what were are—— meant to do.

 CODA

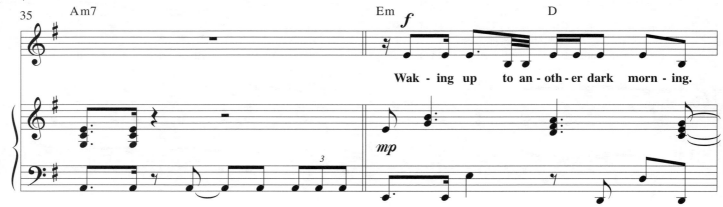

Wak-ing up to an-oth-er dark morn-ing.

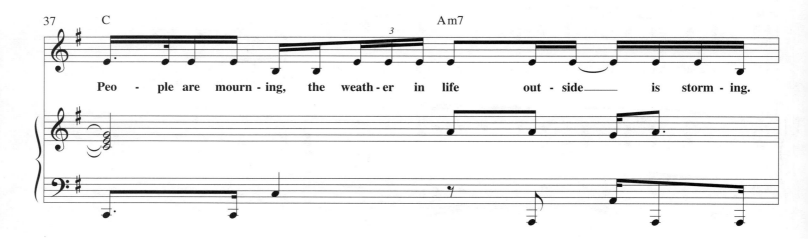

Peo-ple are mourn-ing, the weath-er in life out-side—— is storm-ing.

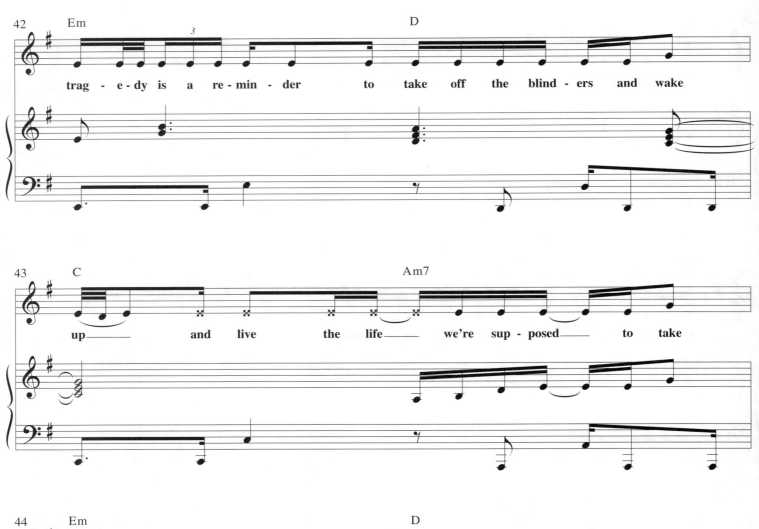

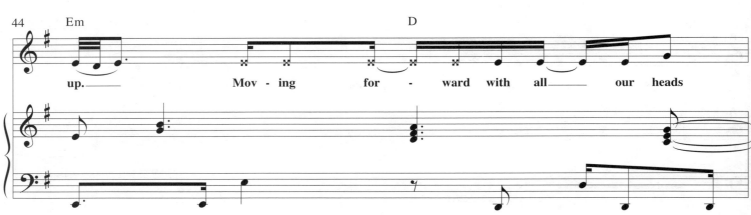

for - give and nev - er give up, 'cause the days we are giv - en are gifts from a - bove. And to -

day we re-mem-ber to live and to love._____ We___ live, we love,___ we

for - give and nev - er give up, 'cause the days we are giv - en are gifts from a - bove. And to -

repeat twice

day we re - mem - ber to live and to love._____

Everything You Ever Wanted

Recorded by Hawk Nelson

Words and Music by
DANIEL BIRO, JASON DUNN
and TREVOR McNEVAN

I walk the line, leave it all be-hind;

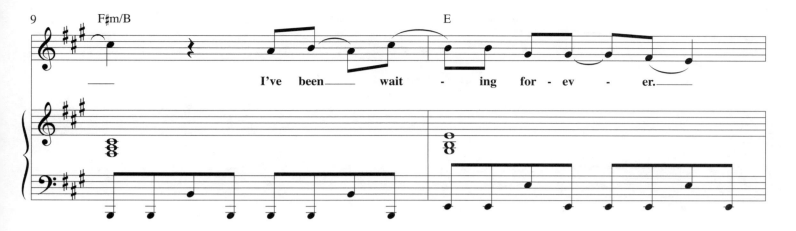

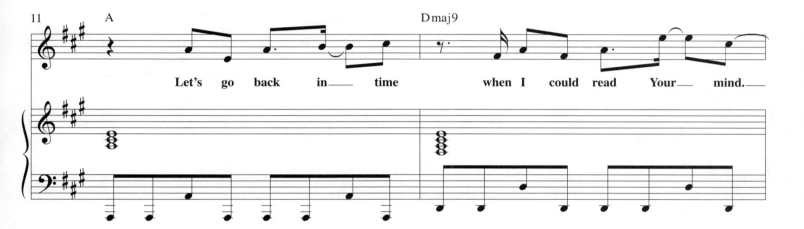

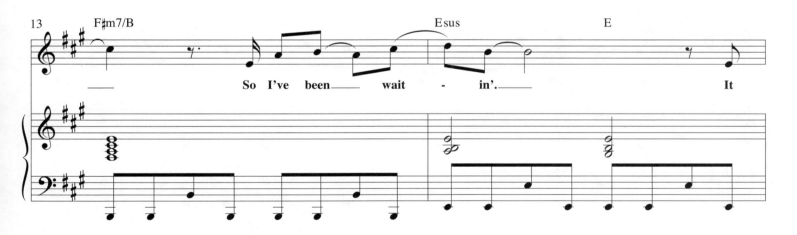

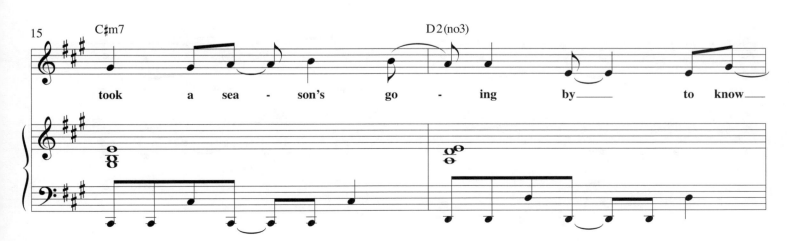

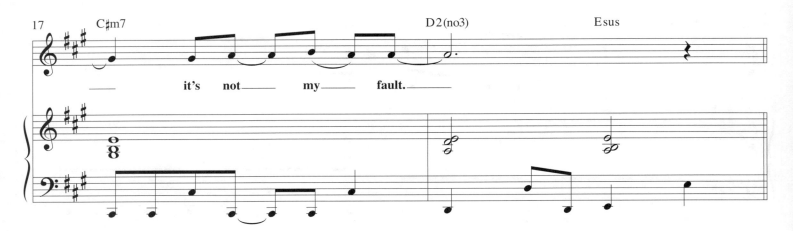

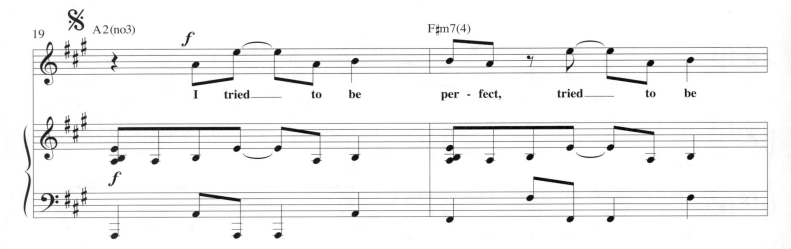

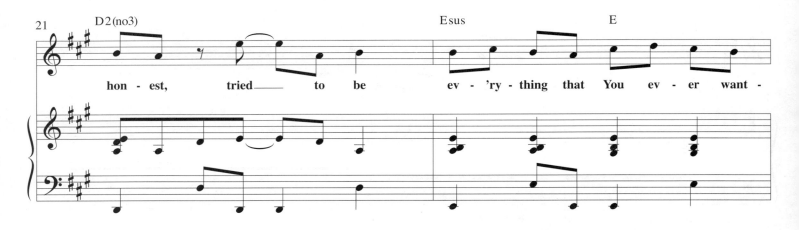

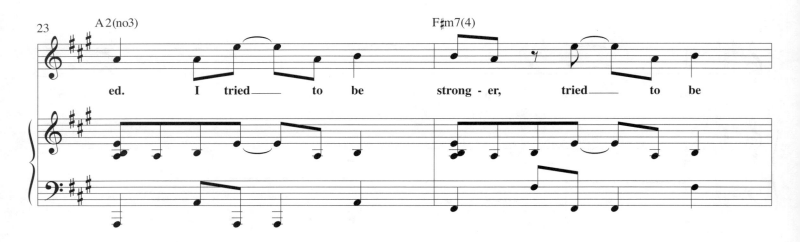

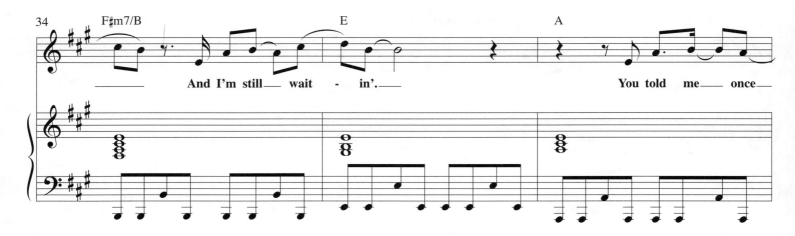

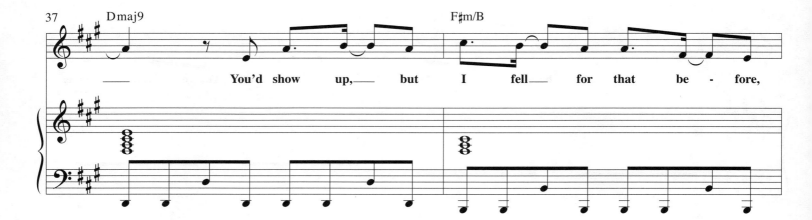

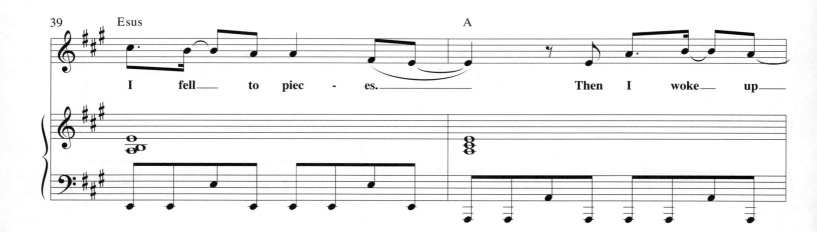

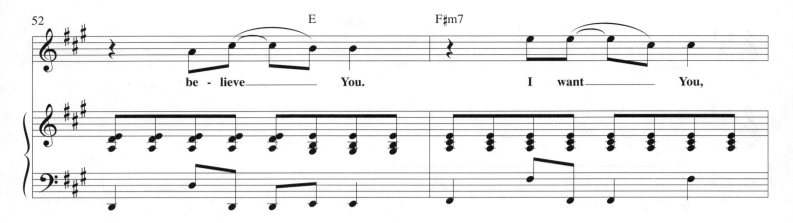

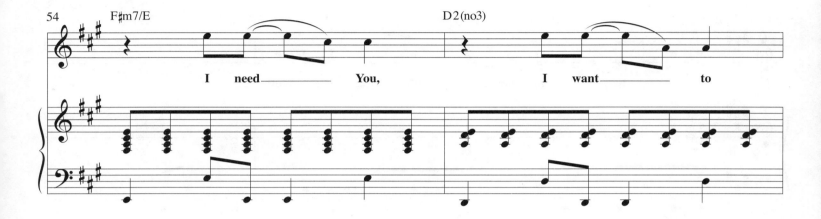

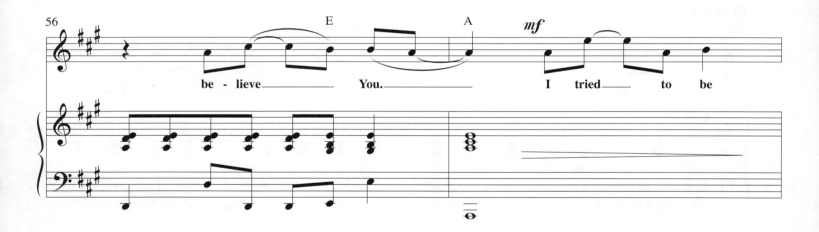

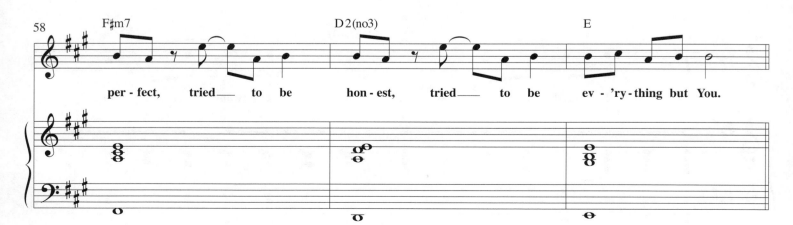

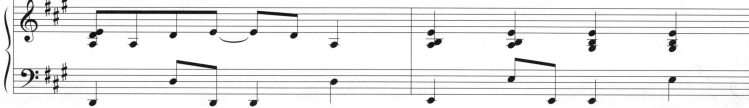

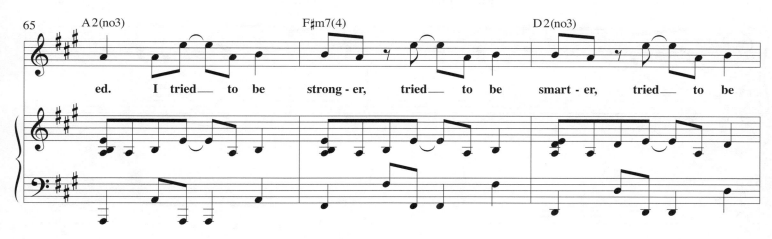

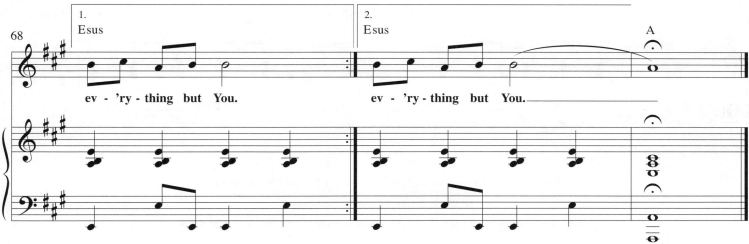

Ready for You

Recorded by Kutless

Words and Music by
JON MICAH SUMRALL

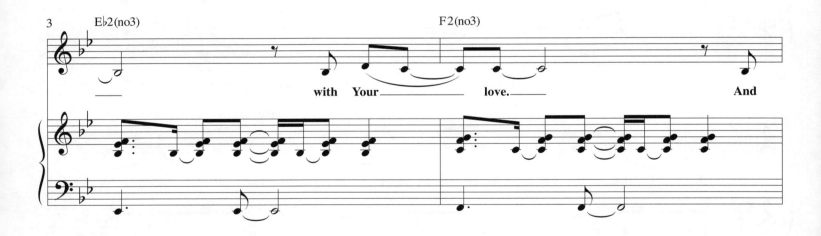

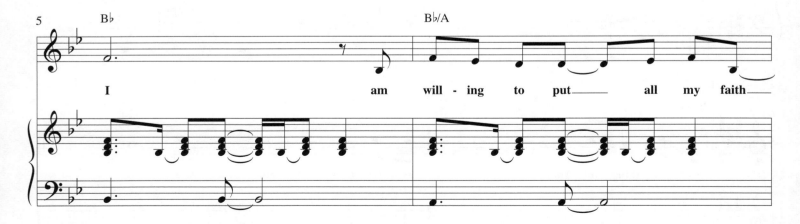

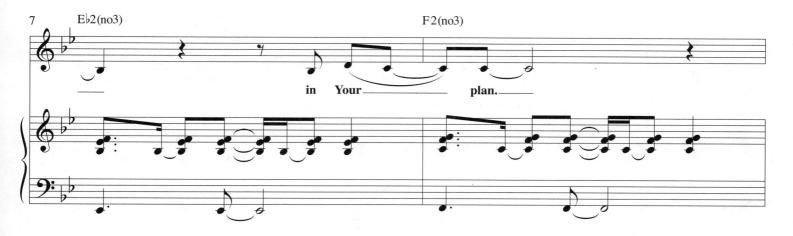

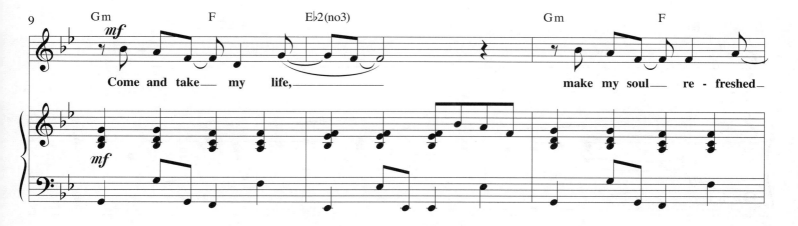

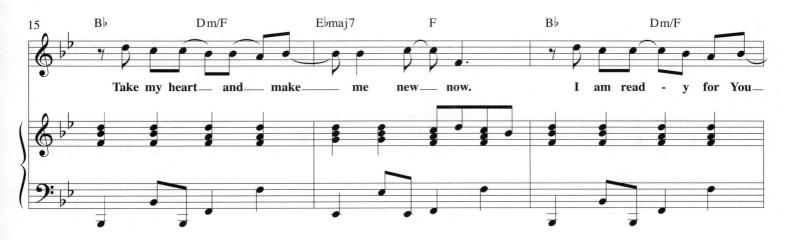

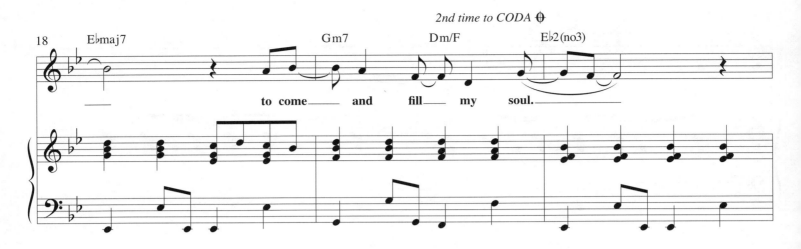

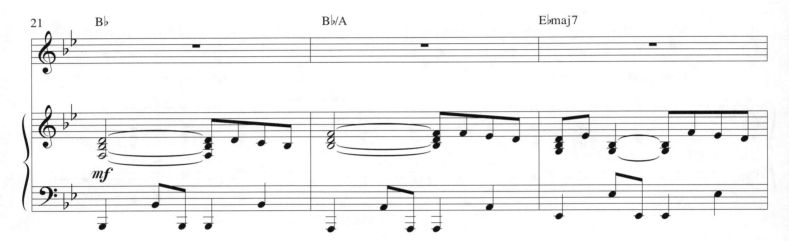

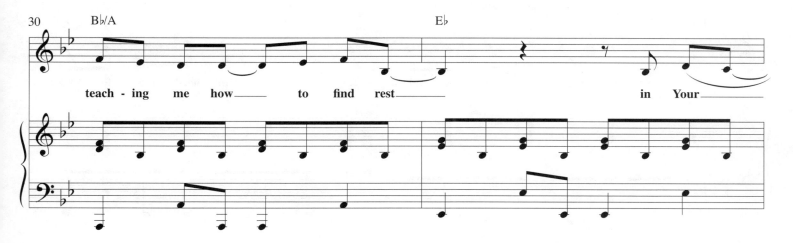

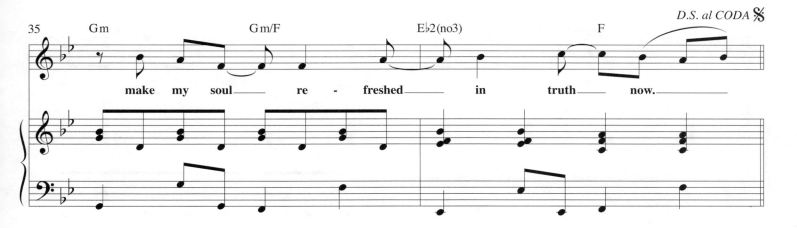

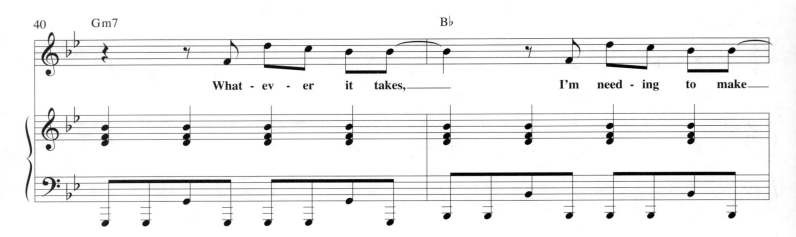

What - ev - er it takes,_____ I'm need - ing to make_____

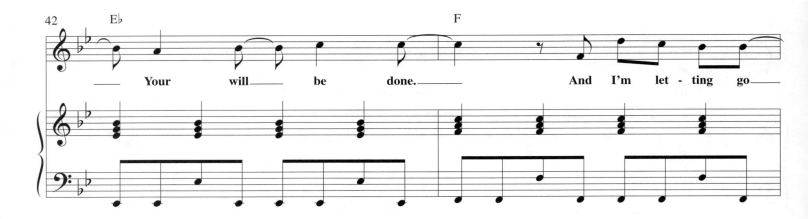

_____ Your will_____ be done._____ And I'm let - ting go_____

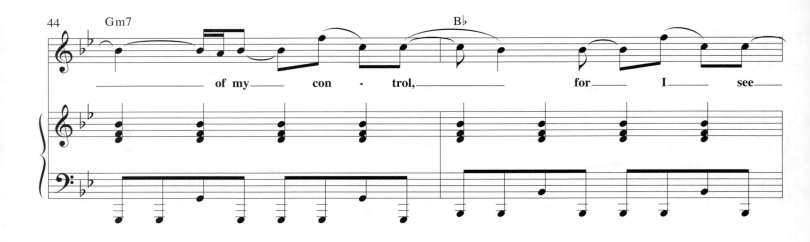

_____ of my_____ con - trol,_____ for_____ I_____ see_____

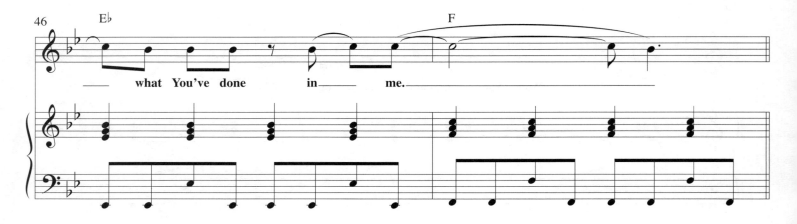

_____ what You've done in_____ me.

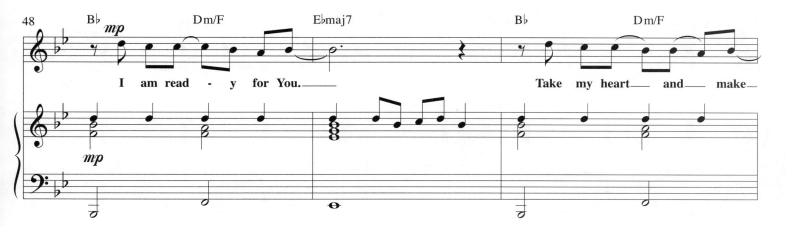

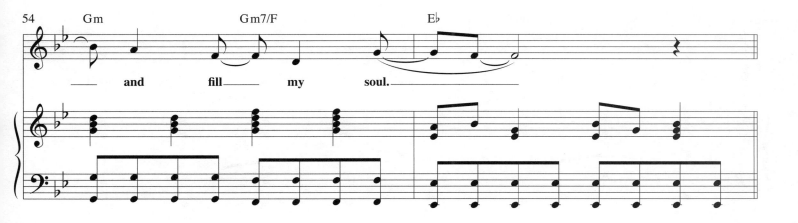

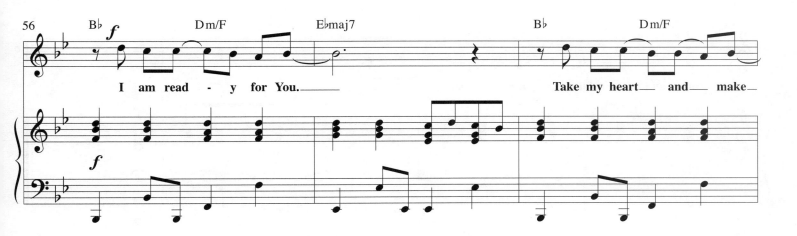

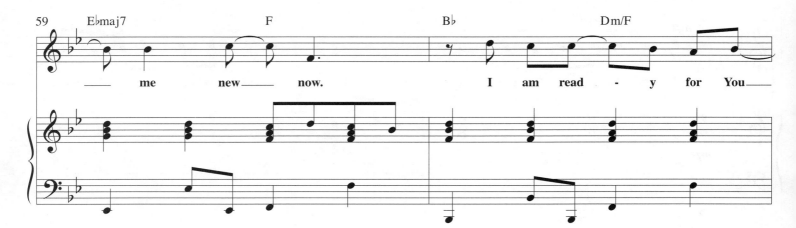

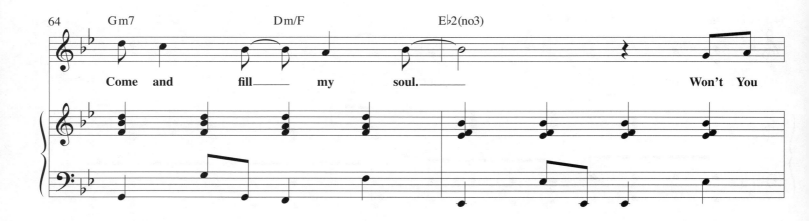

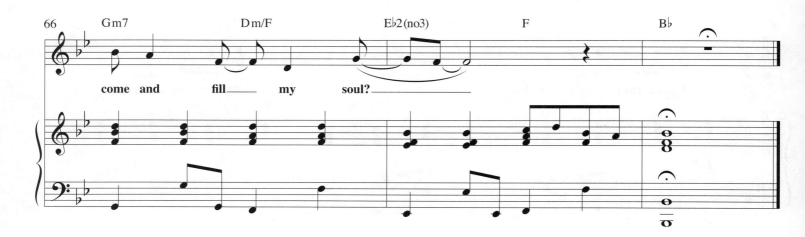

Dead Man (Carry Me)

Recorded by Jars Of Clay

**Words and Music by
DAN HASELTINE, CHARLIE LOWELL,
STEPHEN MASON and MATT ODMARK**

Driving rock ♩ = 128

1. Jan - u - ar - y one, I've got a lot of things on my mind.____
(2.) woke up from a dream a - bout an emp - ty fu - ner - al,____

I'm look - ing at my bod - y through a new spy sat - el - lite.____
but it was bet - ter than a par - ty full of peo - ple I don't real - ly know.____

Try to lift a fin - ger but I
Well, they've got hearts to break and burn,____ dir - ty

don't think I can make a call.____ So
hands____ to____ feel the earth.____ There's

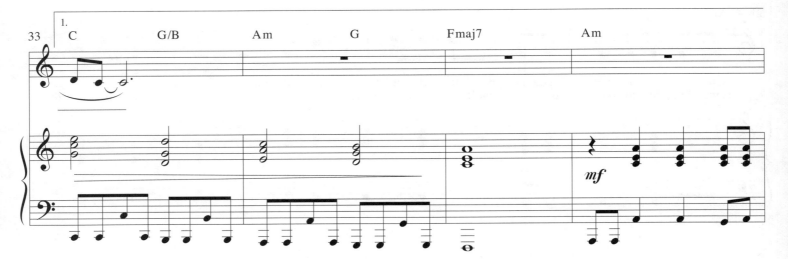

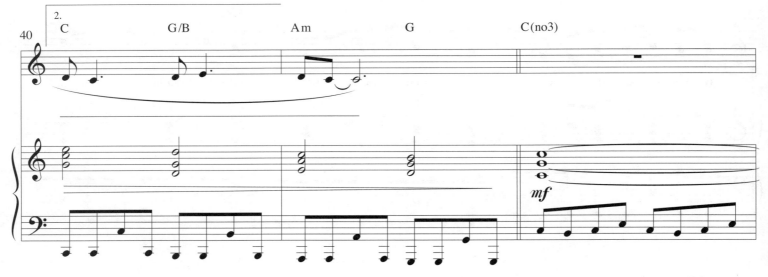

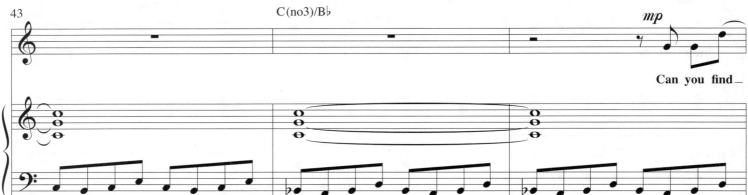

We

Recorded by Joy Williams

**Words and Music by
JOY WILLIAMS and
IAN ESKELIN**

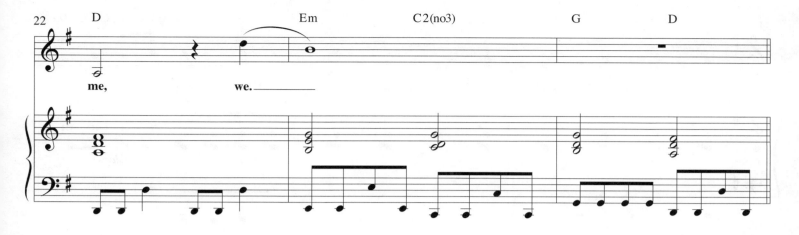

me, we._____

He's on the top of the so - cial scene.___ He's styl - ish, cool and clev -

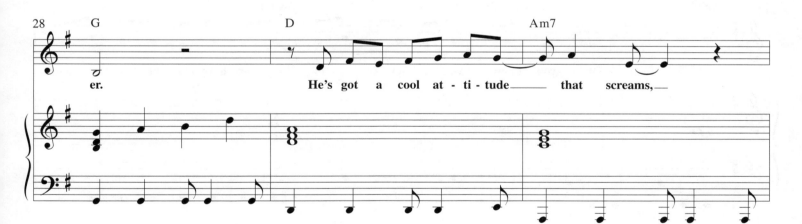

er. He's got a cool at - ti - tude_____ that screams,___

"He's got it all to - geth - er!"_____ You'd think he's ad -

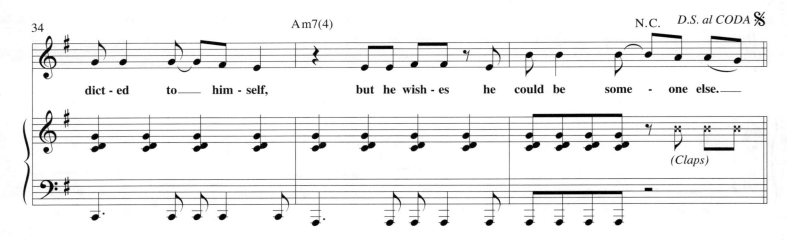

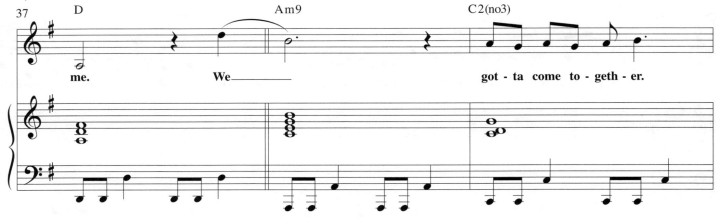

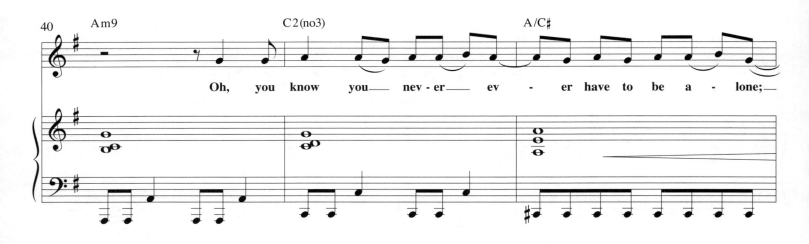

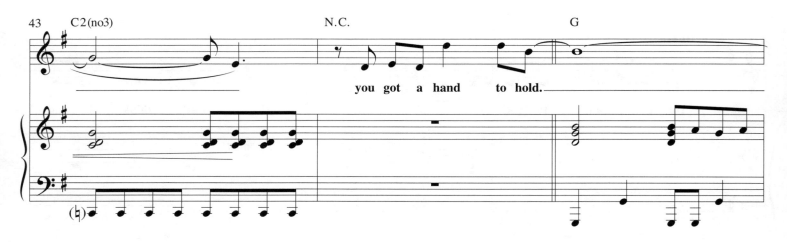

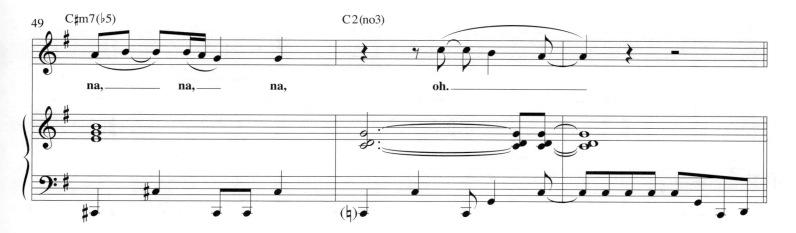

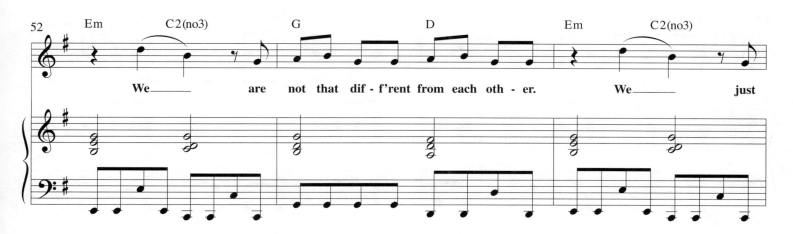

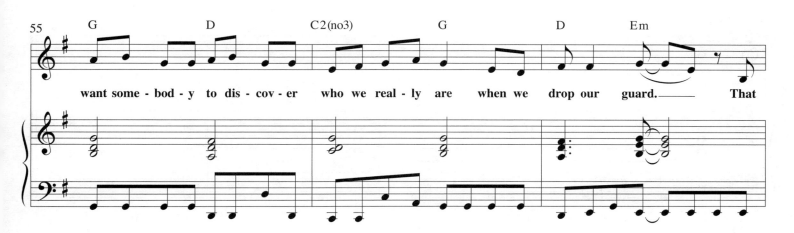

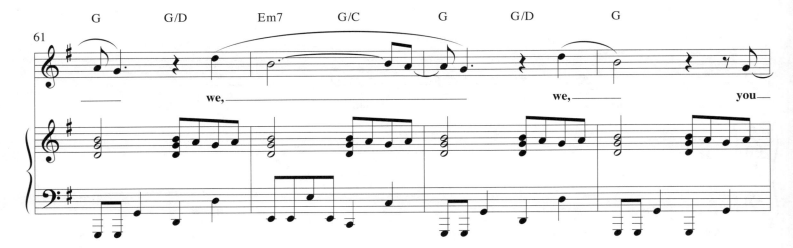

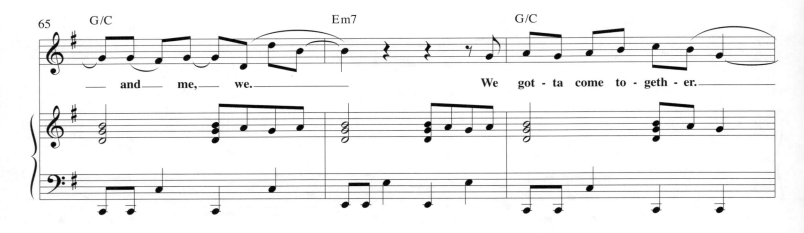

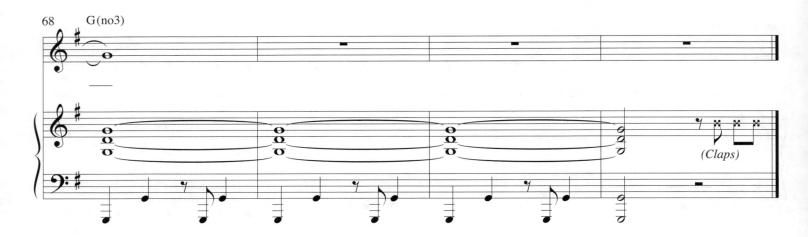

I'm Not Alright

Recorded by Sanctus Real

**Words and Music by
MATT HAMMITT, CHRIS ROHMAN,
MARK GRAALMAN, DAN GARTLEY,
DOUG McKELVEY and CHRISTOPHER STEVEN**

Power ballad ♩ = 67

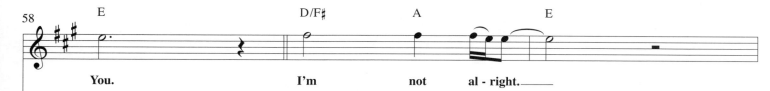

Fearless

Recorded by Building 429

Words and Music by
JASON ROY and JESSE GARCIA

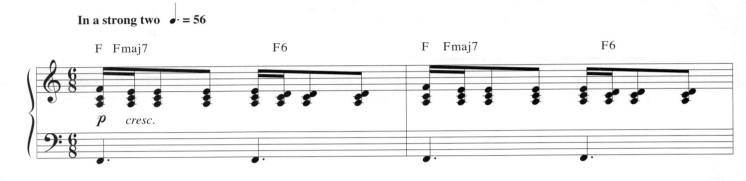

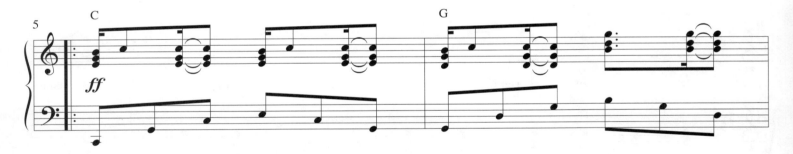

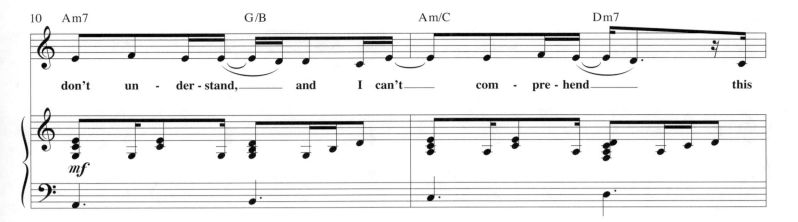

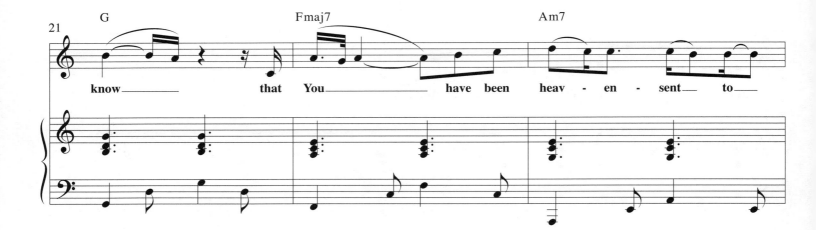

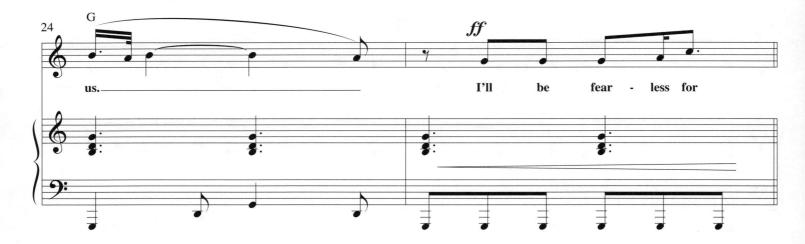

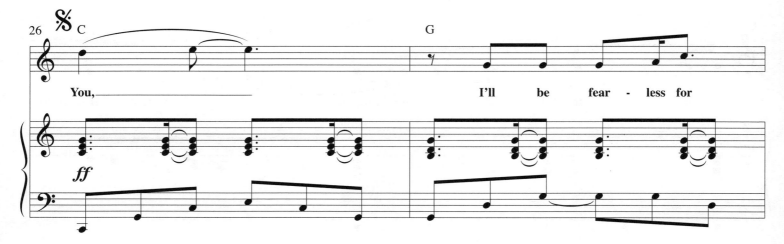

times that I've failed,——— when my doubt has pre-vailed,——— these are the

mo-ments I'm giv-ing to You.——— Be-cause I

can't be a-shamed,— no, I can't——— fear—— the pain——— when it

comes time to be liv-ing proof.——— So the world———

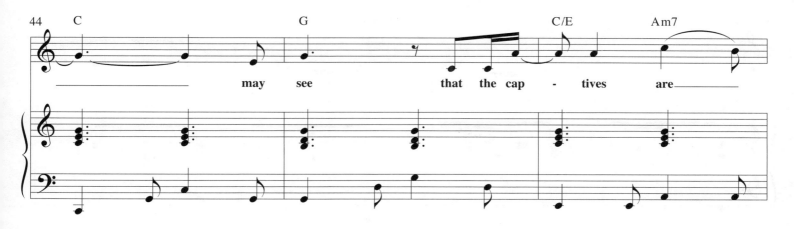

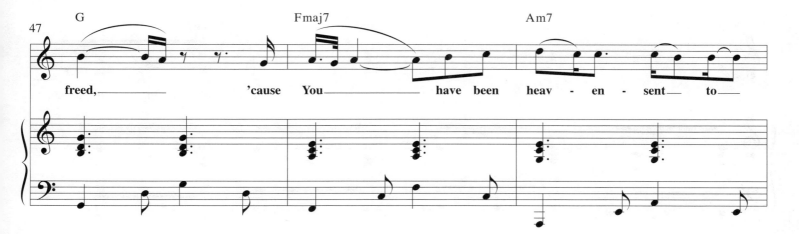

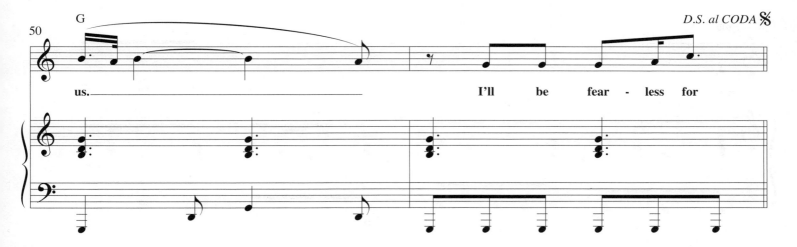

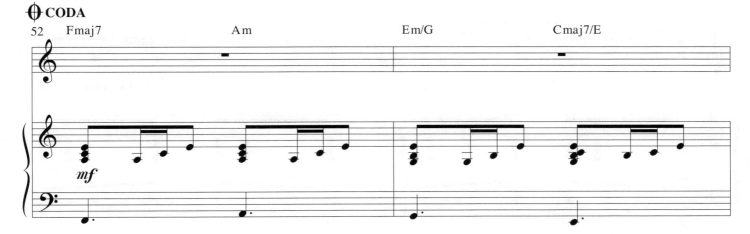

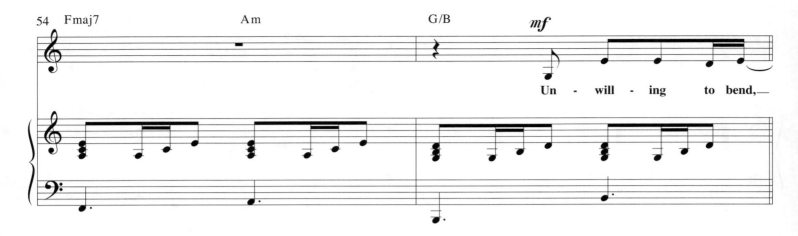

Un - will - ing to bend,—

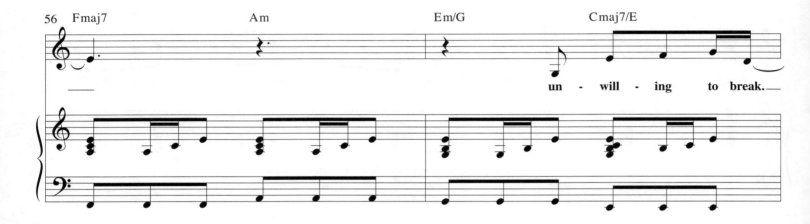

un - will - ing to break.—

And head - strong I'll

stand,————————— no mat - ter what it

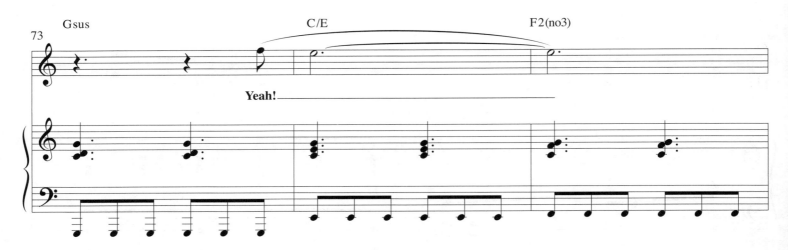

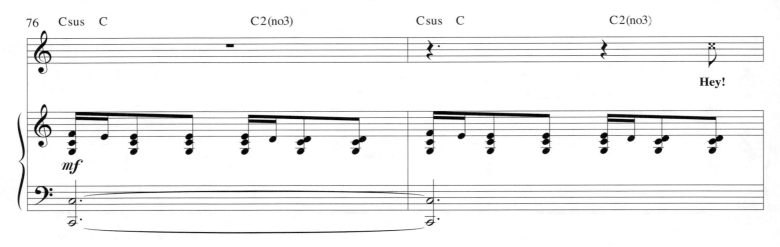

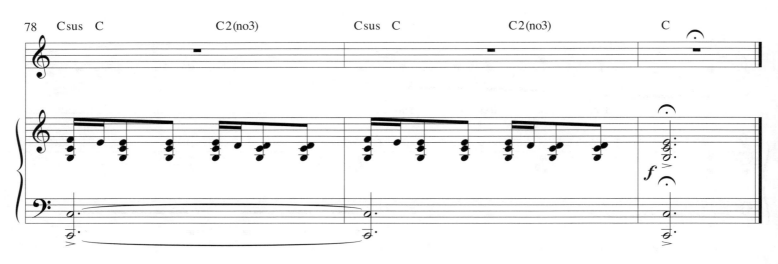

Alive

Recorded by Rebecca St. James

Words and Music by
REBECCA ST. JAMES
and MATT BRONLEEWE

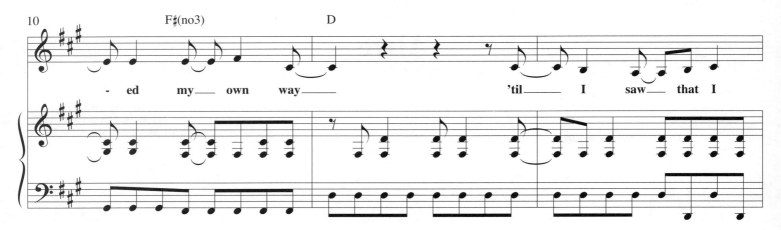

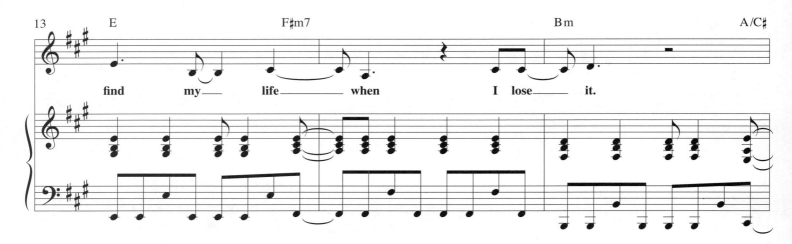

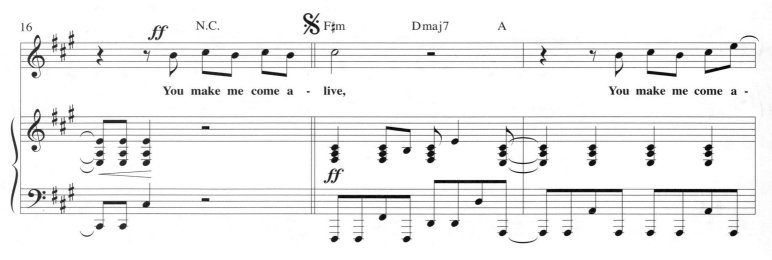

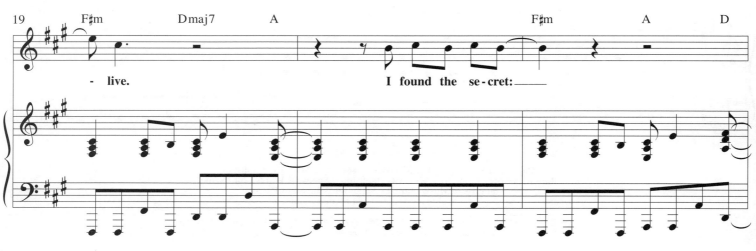

it's on-ly when I let go of what I____ want in____ this life,____

2nd time to CODA

____ You make me come a - live.

I used to think that me,____ my - self____ and____ I

____ were all____ that mat - tered.____ But You showed me all____

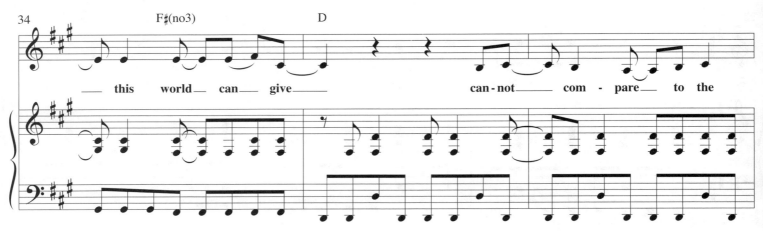

this world can give

can-not com - pare to the

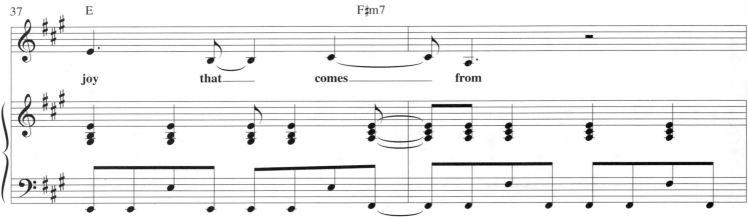

joy that comes from

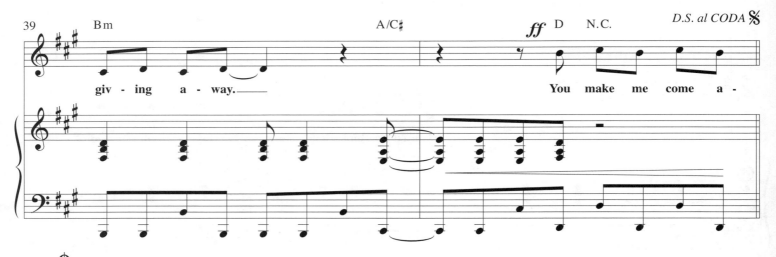

giv - ing a - way. You make me come a -

D.S. al CODA

CODA

And as I fol - low af - ter You,

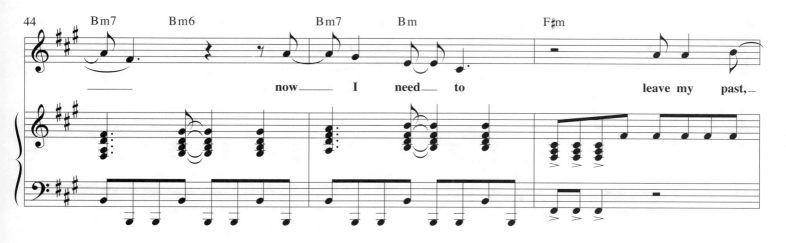

now___ I need__ to leave my past,__

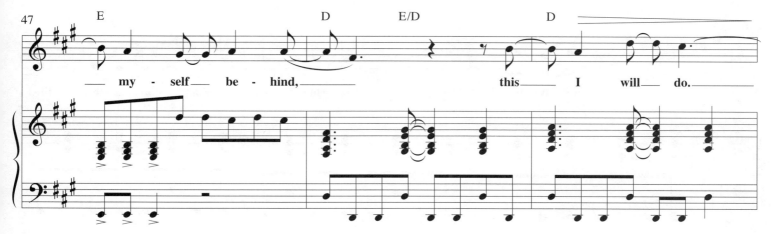

__ my - self__ be - hind,_____ this__ I will__ do.___

You make me come a - live, You make me come a-

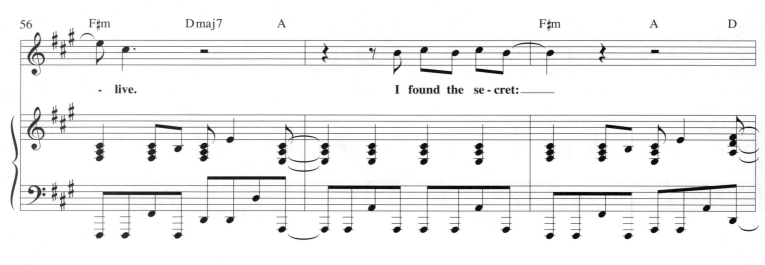

- live. I found the se - cret:_____

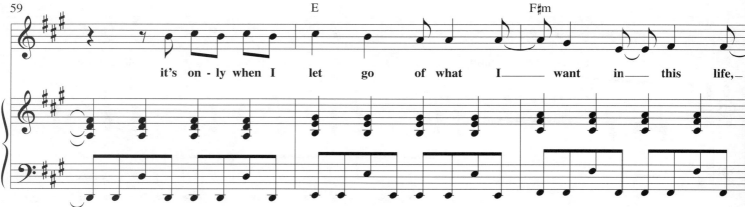

it's on - ly when I let go of what I_____ want in_____ this life,_____

_____ You make me come a - live. (You make_____ me come_____

You make me come a - live. I found the se - cret:_____
_____ a - live.) (You make_____ me come_____ a - live.)

68

F#m A D E

it's on-ly when I let go of what I

(Found the se - cret.)

71

F#m D

want in this life, You make me come a -

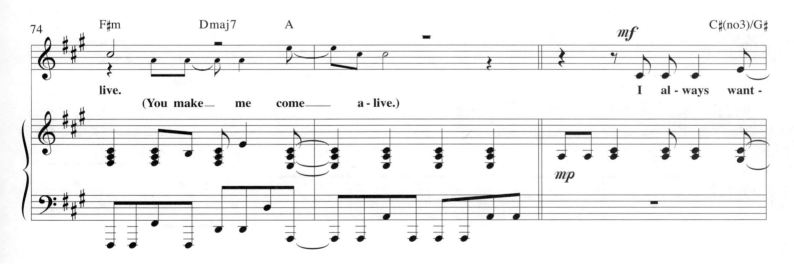

74

F#m Dmaj7 A *mf* C#(no3)/G#

live.

(You make me come a-live.)

I al-ways want-

mp

77

F#(no3) D/F#

-ed to be free 'til I was bound. And then

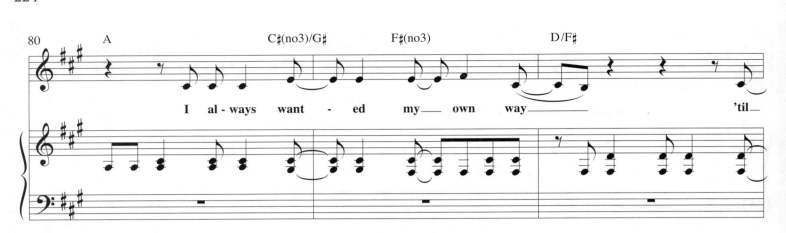

I al - ways want - ed my own way _____ 'til _____

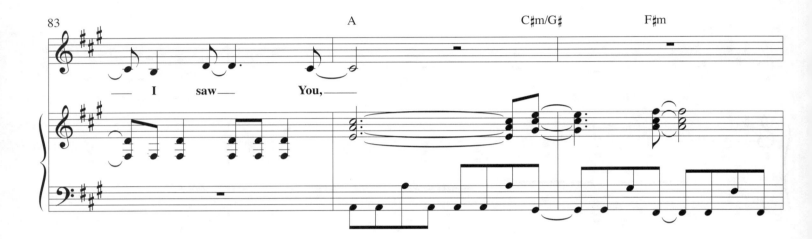

_____ I saw _____ You, _____

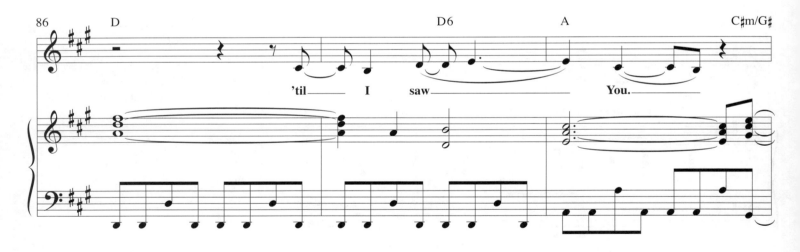

'til _____ I saw _____ You.

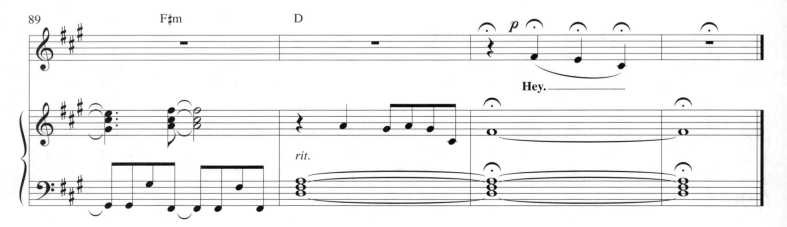

Hey. _____

All That I Am

Recorded by The Afters

Words and Music by
**MARC DODD, MATT FUQUA,
JOSH HAVENS and BRAD WIGGERS**

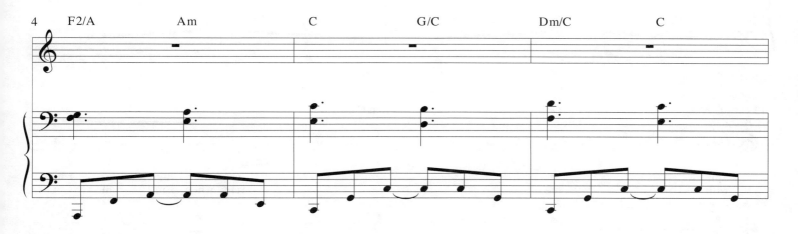

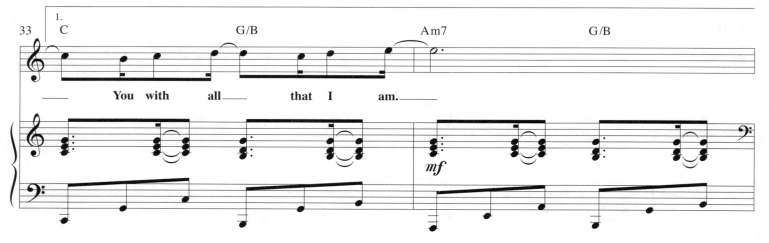

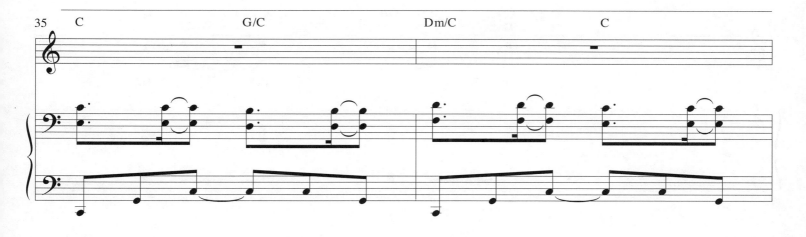

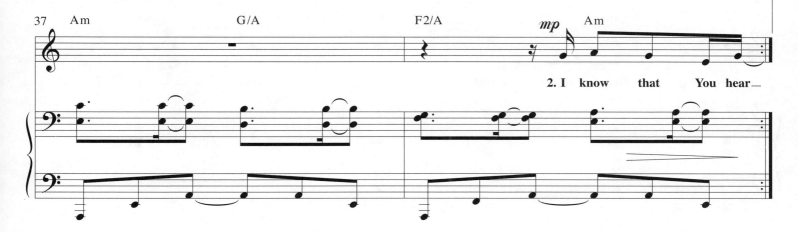

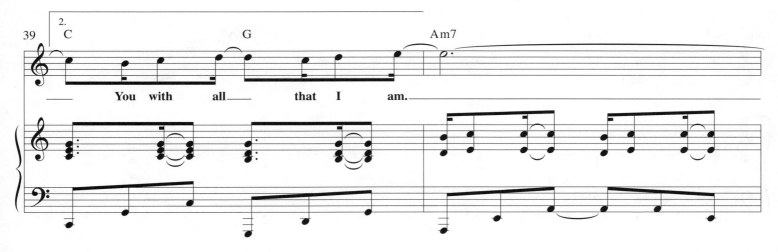

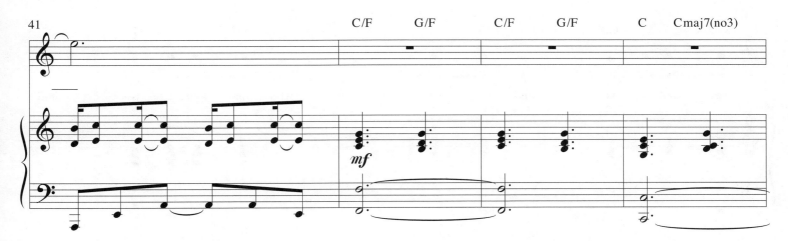

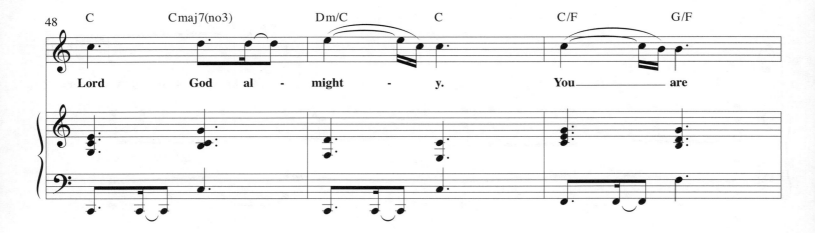

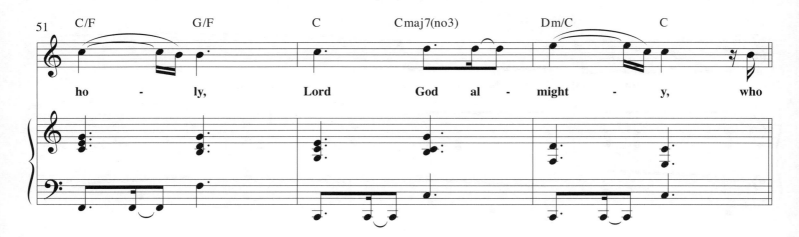

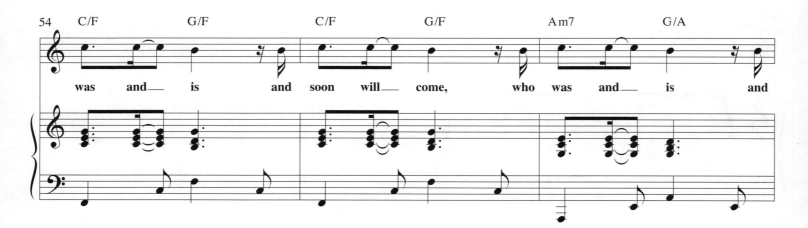

soon will come. Who was and is and soon will come, who

was and is and soon will come. Lord, You are, and

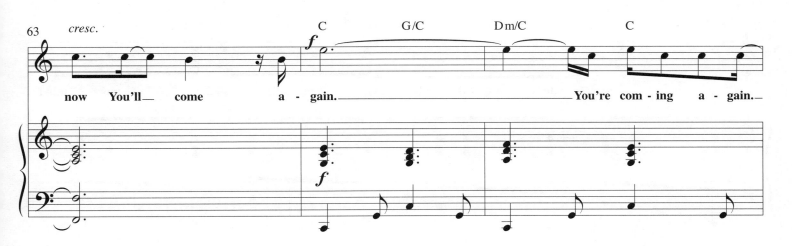

cresc.

now You'll come a - gain. You're com - ing a - gain.

Just like You said,

232

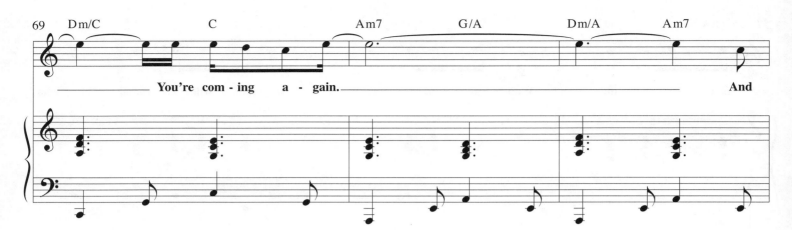

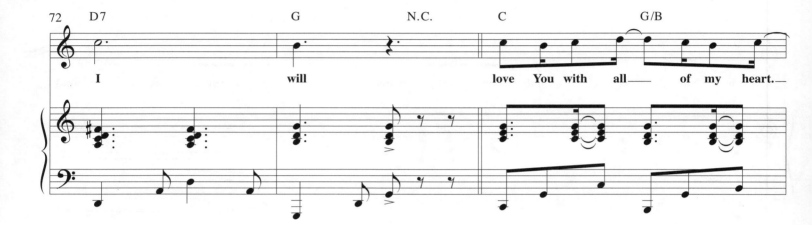

Je - sus, I'll love_____ You with all_____ that I am._____

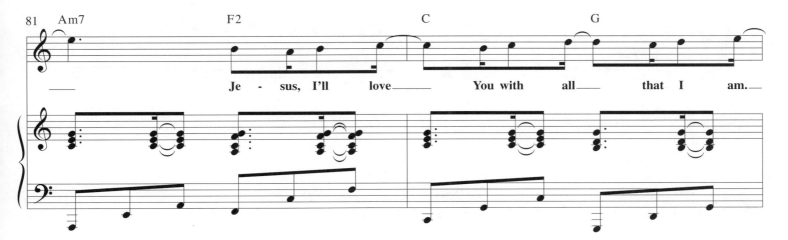

Je - sus, I'll love_____ You with all_____ that I am._____

Je - sus, I'll love_____ You with all_____ that I am._____

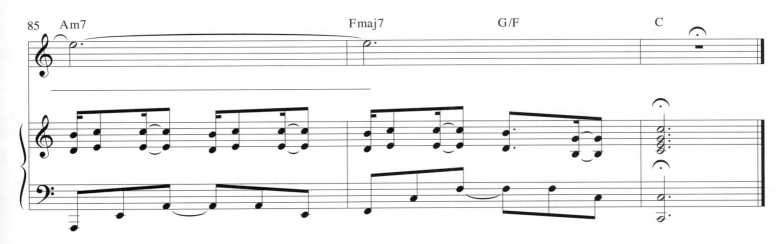

Free

Recorded by Shawn McDonald

Words and Music by
SHAWN McDONALD and WILL HUNT

And all this ex - pec - ta - tion on —

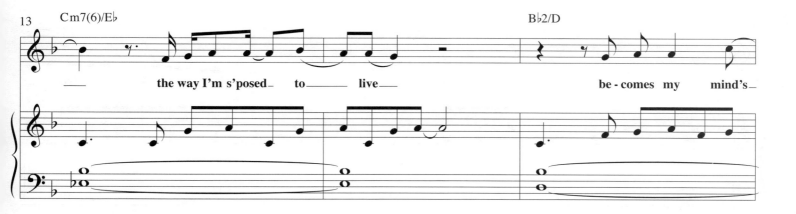

the way I'm s'posed to live — be - comes my mind's —

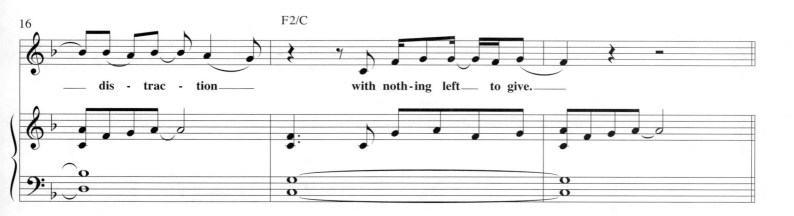

dis - trac - tion — with noth-ing left to give. —

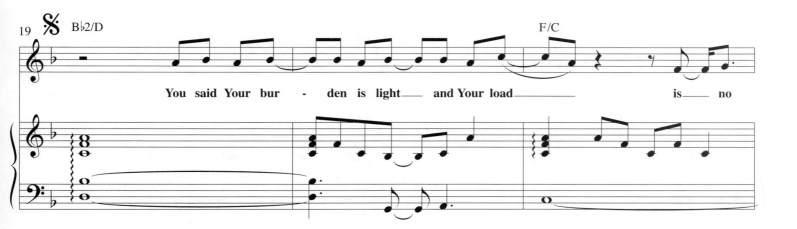

You said Your bur - den is light — and Your load — is — no

more.

You said Your ways are right and in

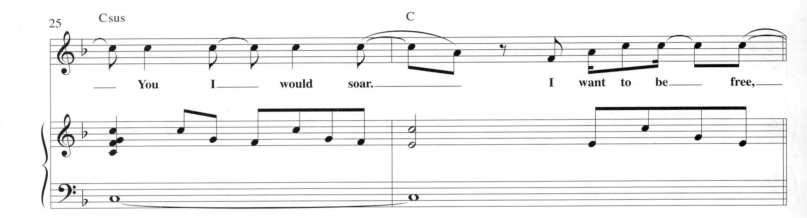

You I would soar. I want to be free,

free to dance and free to sing,

free to live and love and free, oh, free to be me.

2nd time to CODA

I feel like my heart

Cm6/E♭

is be - ing beat down in - to the ground.

B♭2/D

F2/C

In You I'm long - ing for some peace to be found.

F2

I know the heav - i - ness that's

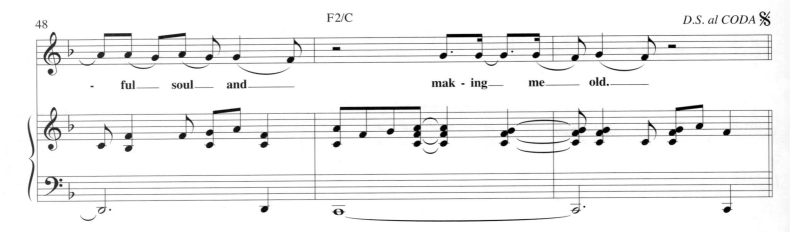

oh, free to be me.

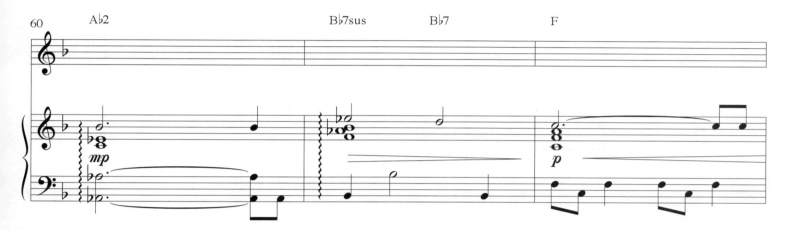

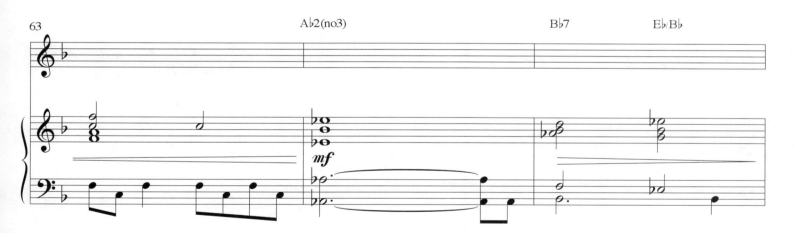

I want to be free,

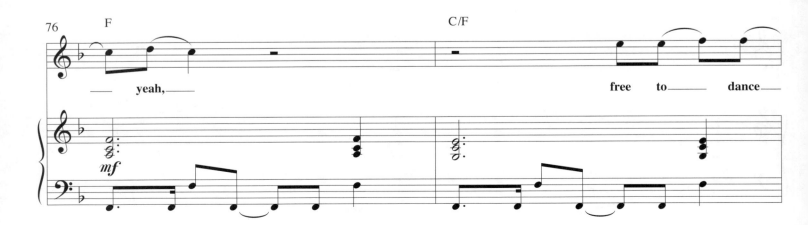

and free— to sing,—————— free to live—— and love—— and free,—

— oh,—— free—— to be me.——————

Fade to end

Free.

mp

Fade to end

Play repeat 3 times

pp

Fire

Recorded by Krystal Meyers

Words and Music by
**KRYSTAL MEYERS, IAN ESKELIN,
ANDREW BOJANIC and ELIZABETH HOOPER**

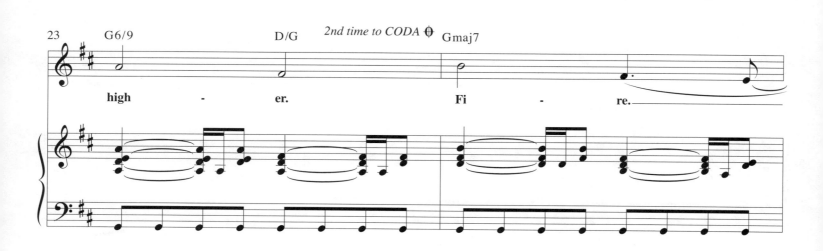

Let__ Your fi - re feed_____ on all__ my dis - be - lief,__

'cause You are all__ I need;__ You're__ con - ta - gious.

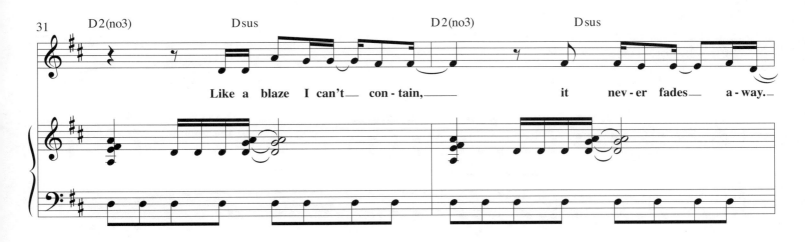

Like a blaze I can't__ con - tain,_____ it nev - er fades__ a - way.__

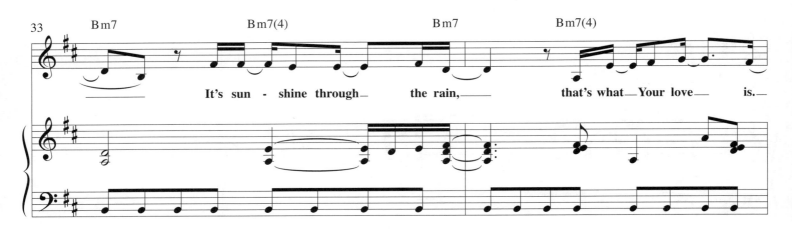

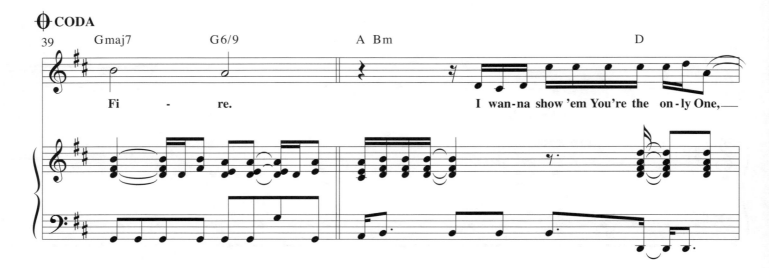

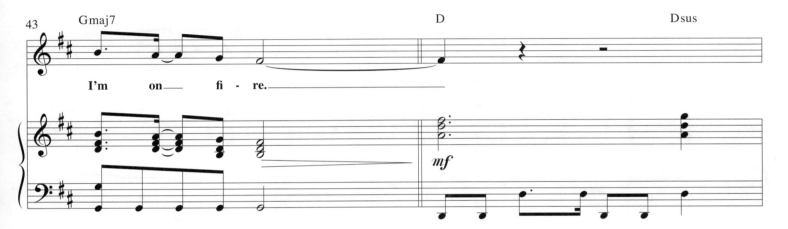

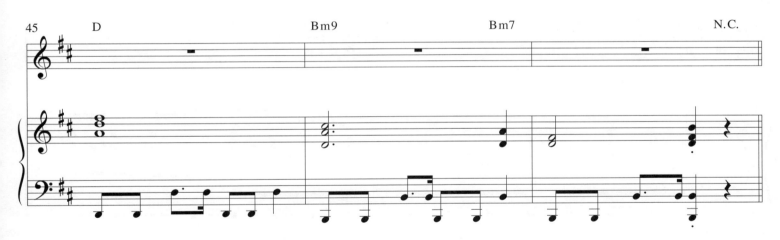

I Can't Do This

Recorded by Plumb

Words and Music by
TIFFANY LEE ARBUCKLE
and MATT BRONLEEWE

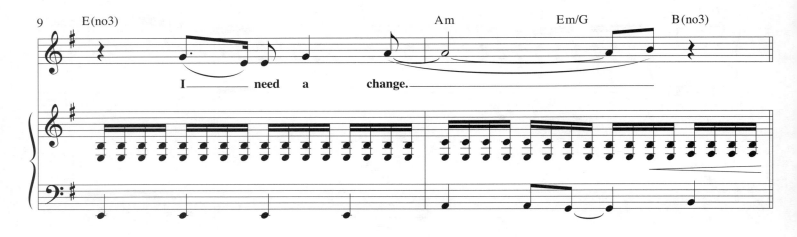

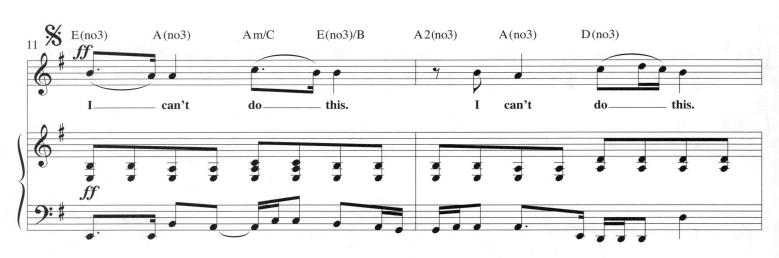

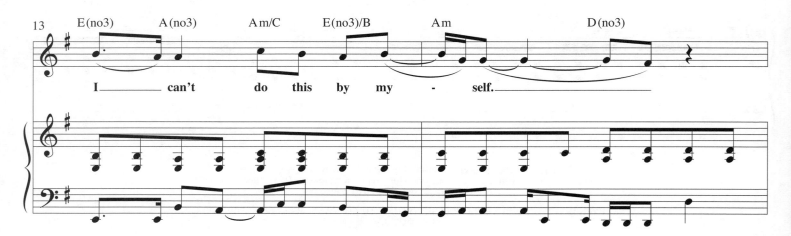

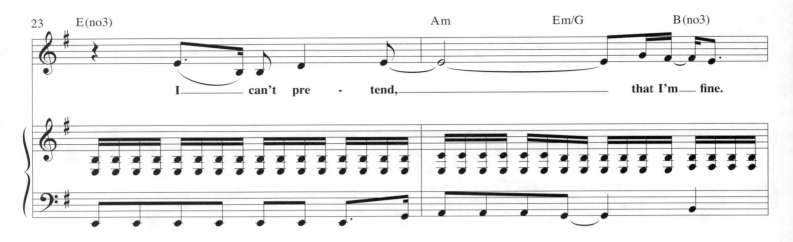

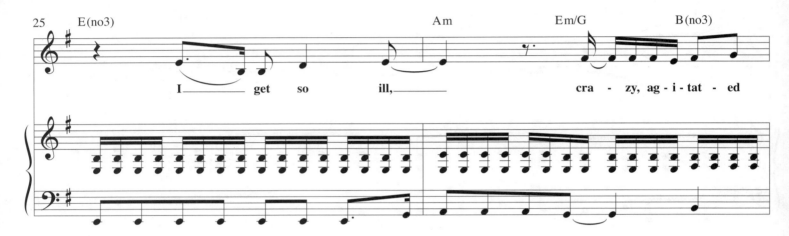

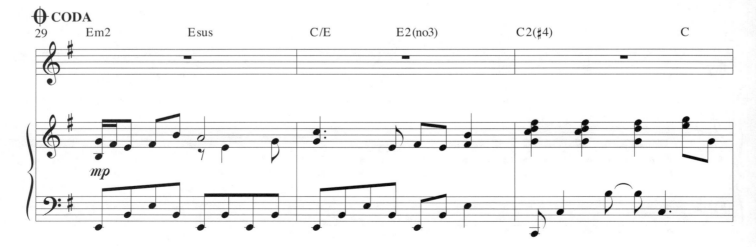

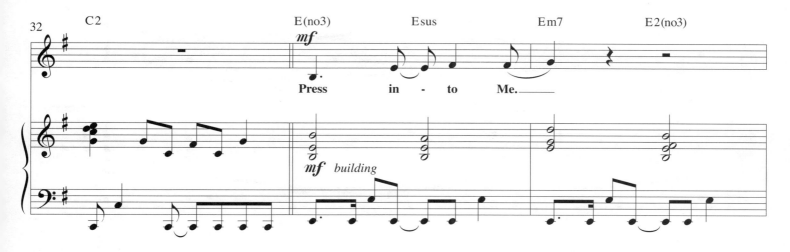

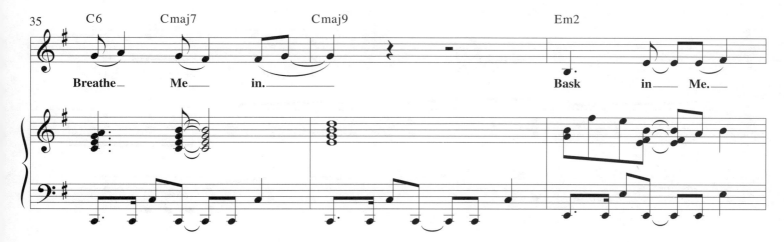

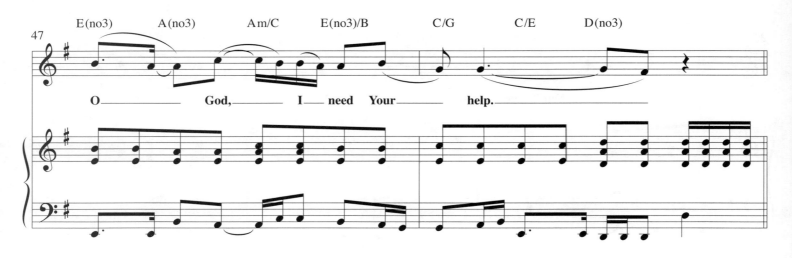

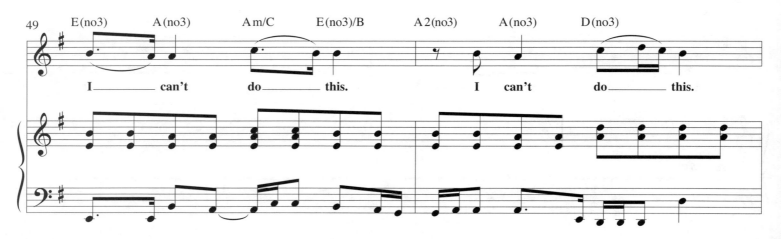

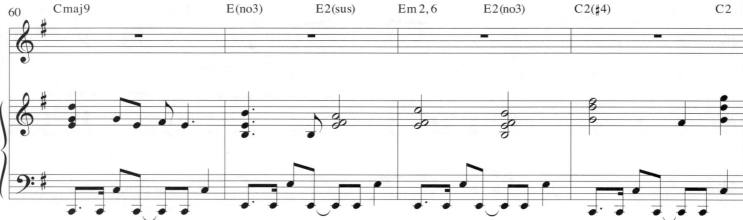

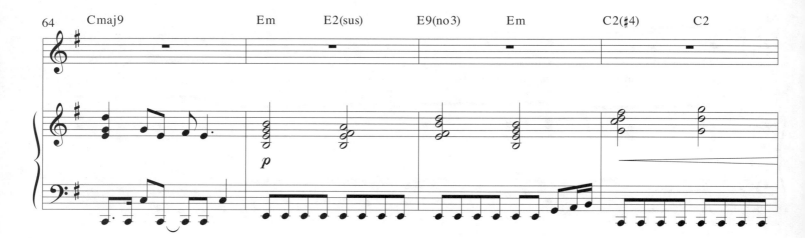

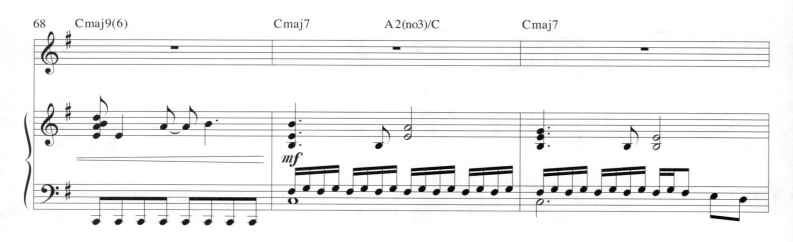

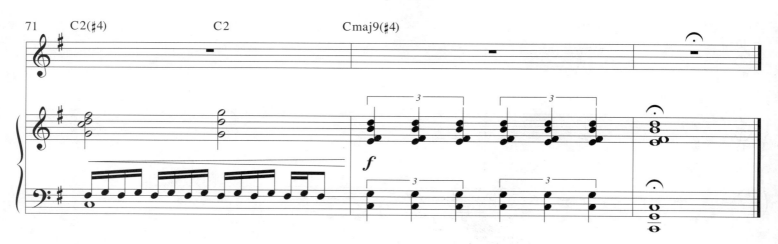

Sound of Melodies

Recorded by Leeland

Words and Music by
LEELAND DAYTON MOORING, STEVE WILSON
and JACK ANTHONY MOORING

With joy ♩. = 69

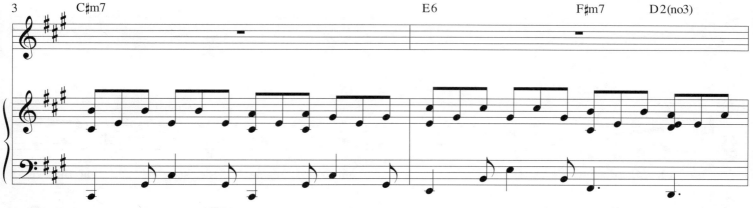

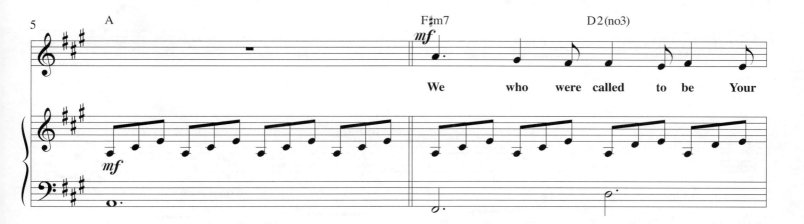

We who were called to be Your

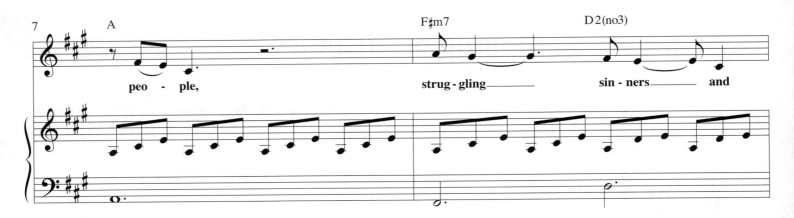

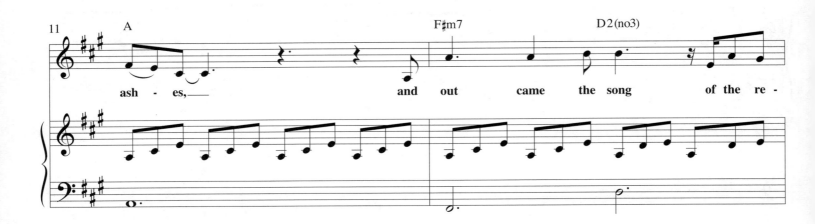

deemed.   Can You hear   the

sound   of mel - o - dies,   oh,   the   sound   of mel - o - dies   ris - ing

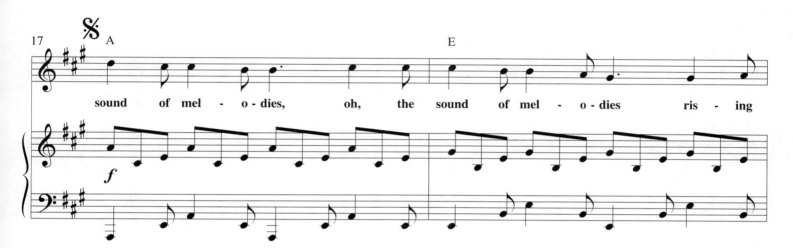

up   to   You,   ris - ing   up   to   You,   God?   The

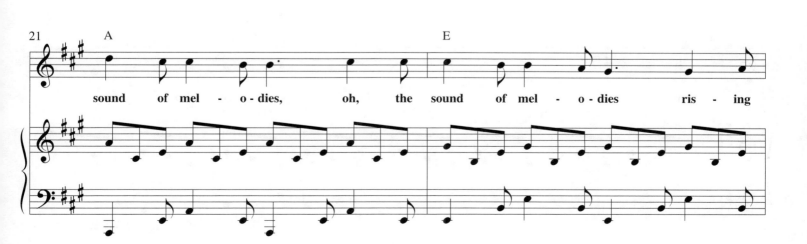

sound   of mel - o - dies,   oh,   the   sound   of mel - o - dies   ris - ing

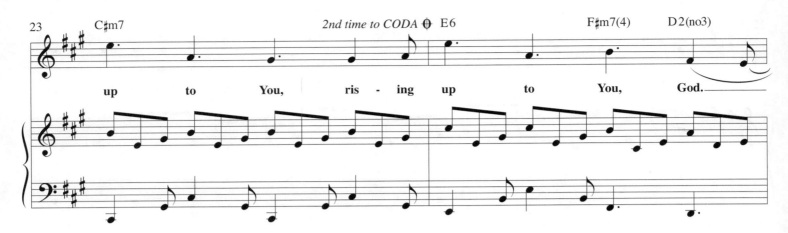

-va - tion, it fills Your daugh - ters and Your

sons, Your daugh - ters and Your—

— sons. Can You hear the

CODA

up to You, God. The sound of Your love, the sound of Your

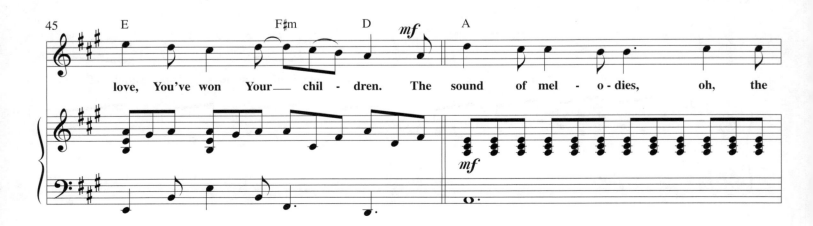

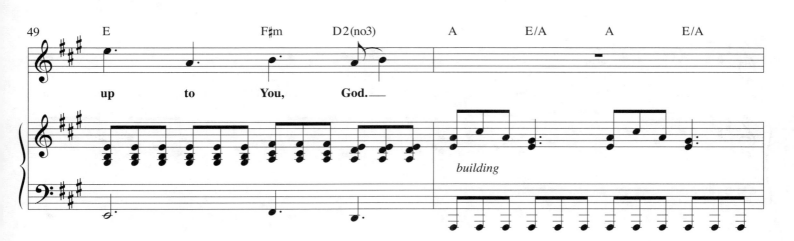

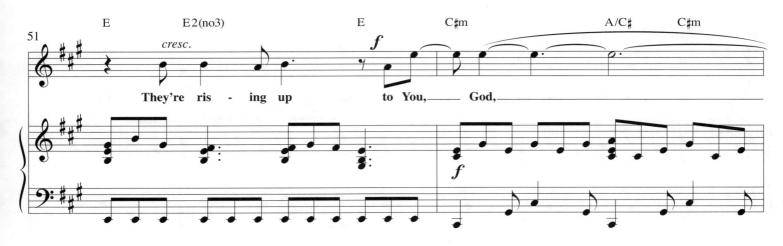

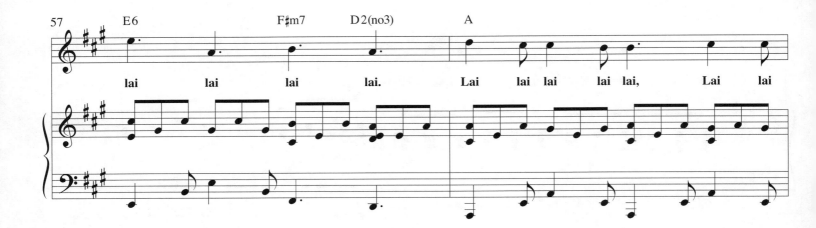

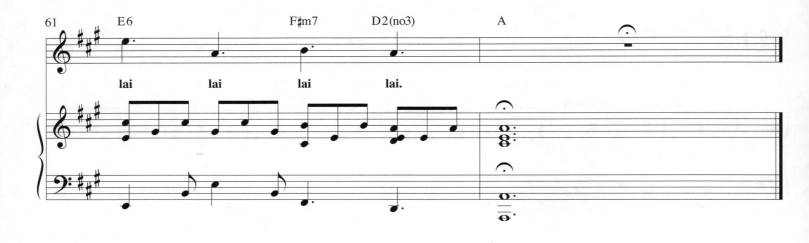

Can't Go On

Recorded by Group 1 Crew

**Words and Music by
JOSE "MAXWELL" REYES, PABLO VILLATORO,
CHRIS STEVENS and BENJAHMEN "YoungLyon.net" THOM**

Spoken: **I can't go on without You.**

I've tried so many times, and I've failed.

Lord, I real-ly need You in my life;___ fall ev-'ry time that You're not in

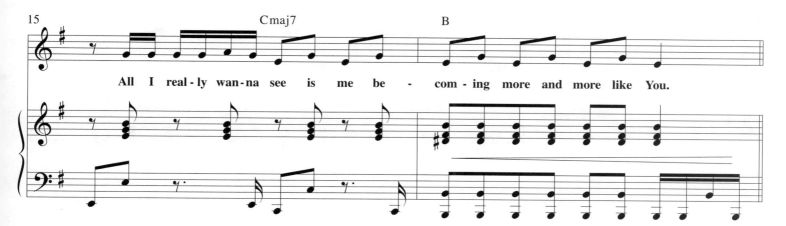

All I real-ly wan-na see is me be-com-ing more and more like You.

Lord, I real-ly need You in my life;_____ fall ev-'ry time that You're not in

sight. Can't go on with-out Your love,_____ I can't go on.

And I don't wan-na face this world a-lone,_____ I don't wan-na do this on my

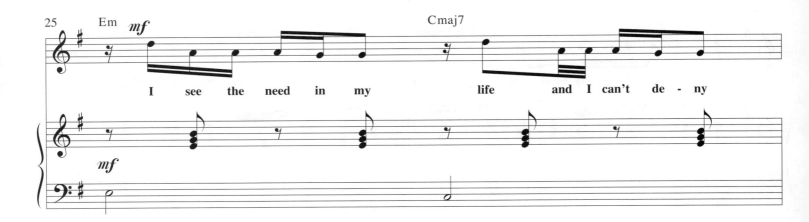

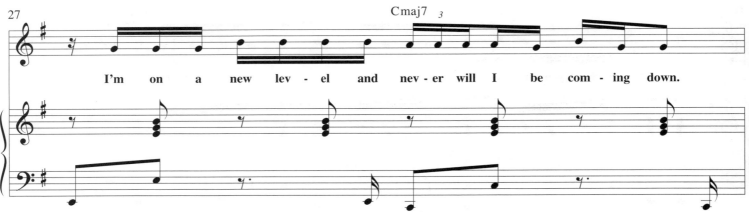

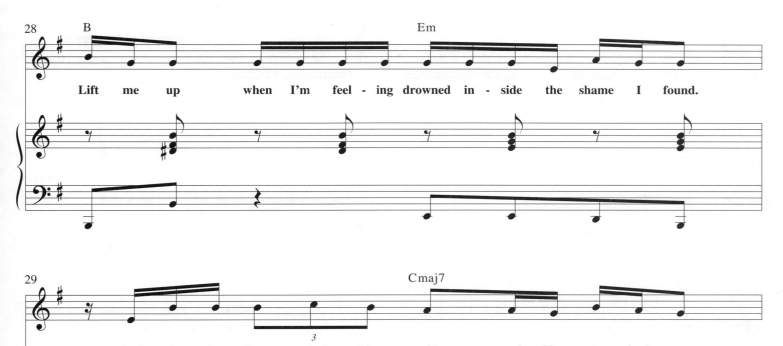

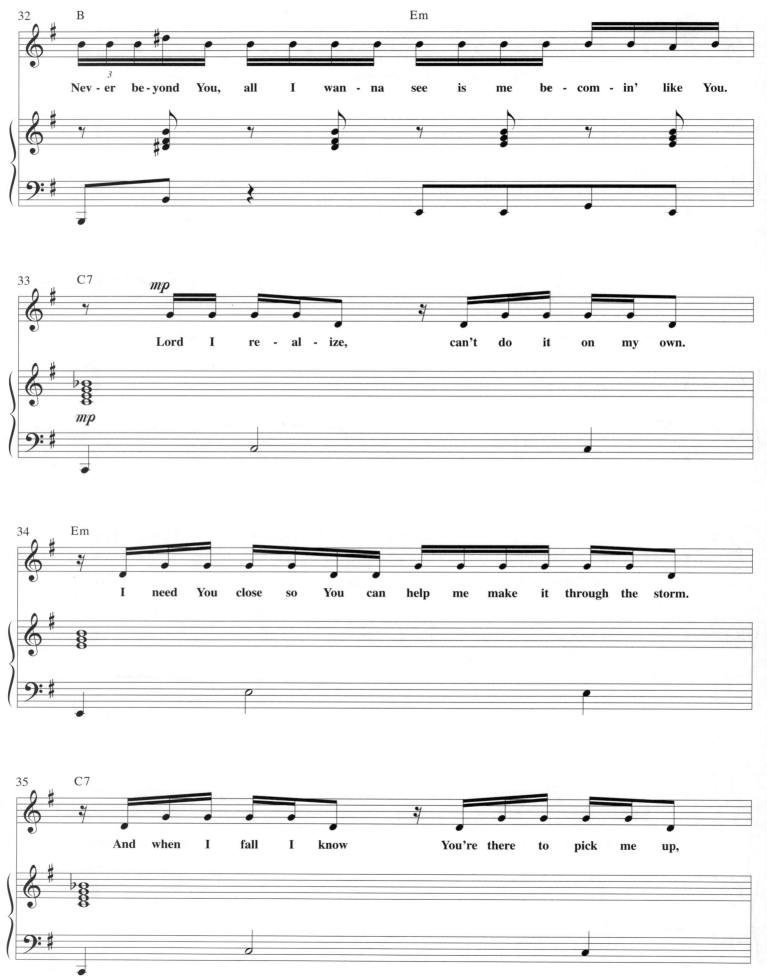

brush me off, and then You're quick to bring me back in - side Your love.

I don't know where to go now; I'm lost in this e - mo -

tion. I'm giv - in' You con - trol now. Pull me up from the bot - tom of the o - cean.

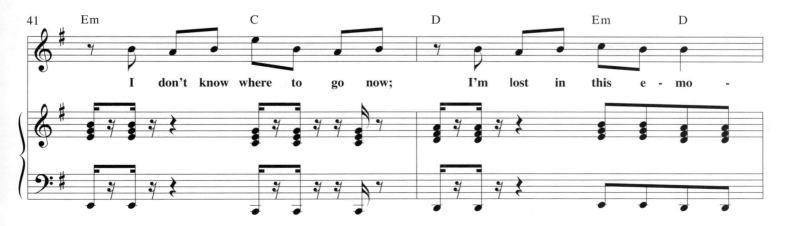

I don't know where to go now; I'm lost in this e - mo -

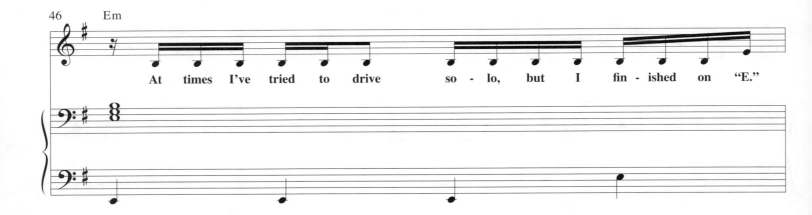

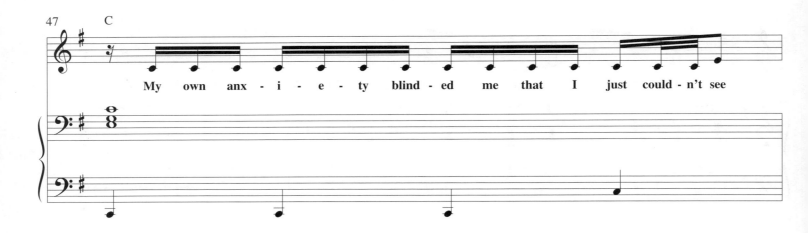

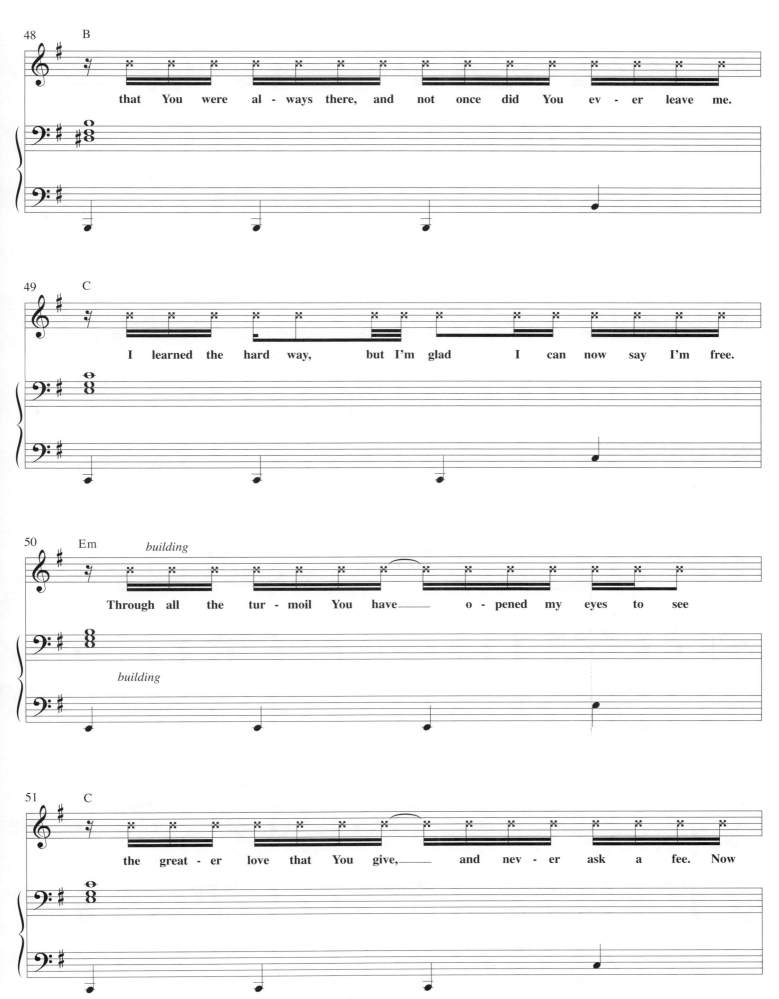

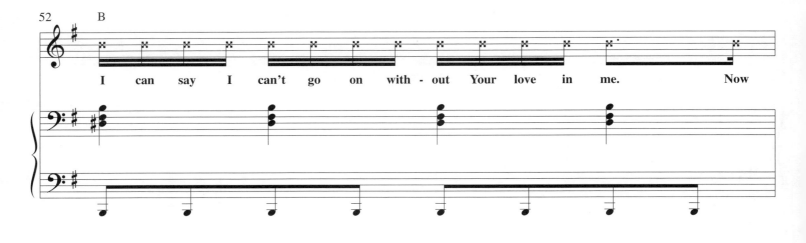

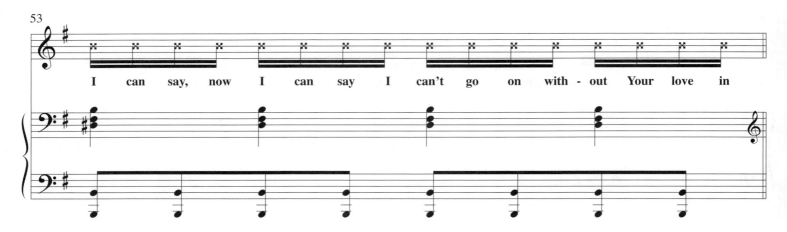

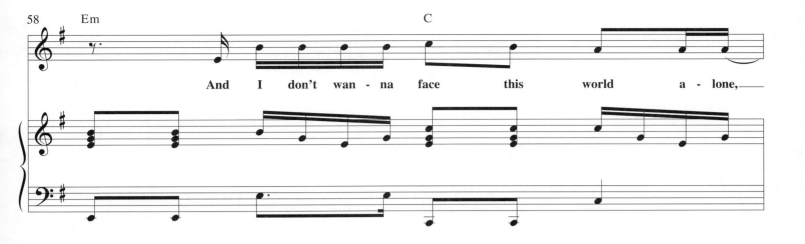

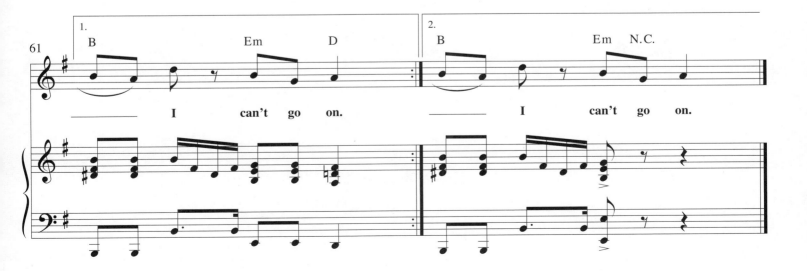

OTHER ARTIST RELATED
FOLIOS

The following songs are also available in the artist folios listed:

ALIVE (Rebecca St. James)
Available in the songbook "If I Had One Chance to Tell You Something"
Hal Leonard (HL00306770)

ALL THAT I AM (The Afters)
Available in the songbook "I Wish We All Could Win"
Hal Leonard (HL08739859)

BURN FOR YOU (tobyMac)
Available in the songbook "Welcome to Diverse City"
Hal Leonard (HL00306694)

CRY OUT TO JESUS (Third Day)
Available in the songbook "Wherever You Are"
Hal Leonard (HL00306766)

DEAD MAN (CARRY ME) (Jars of Clay)
Available in the songbook "Good Monsters"
Brentwood-Benson Music Publishing (4575713117)

FEARLESS (Building 429)
Available in the songbook "Fearless"
Word Music (080689 512285)

FIRE (Krystal Meyers)
Available in the songbook "Krystal Meyers"
Brentwood-Benson Music Publishing (4575711397)

HELD (Natalie Grant)
Available in the songbook "Awaken"
Shawnee Press (747510075110)

HERE I AM (Michael W. Smith)
Available in the songbook "Healing Rain"
Word Music (080689 492280)

HOW GREAT IS OUR GOD (Chris Tomlin)
Available in the songbook "Arriving"
worshiptogether (SB54680)

I AM (Mark Schultz)
Available in the songbook "Live . . . A Night of Stories & Songs"
Word Music (080689 496288)

LET GO (BarlowGirl)
Available in the songbook "Another Journal Entry"
Word Music 080689 504280)

LIFESONG (Casting Crowns)
Available in the songbook "Lifesong"
Hal Leonard (HL00306748)

MY SAVIOR, MY GOD (Aaron Shust)
Available in the songbook "Anything Worth Saying"
Brentwood-Benson Music Publishing (4575712857)

READY FOR YOU (Kutless)
Available in the songbook "Strong Tower"
Hal Leonard (HL00306726)

SO LONG SELF (MercyMe)
Available in the songbook "Coming Up to Breathe"
Hal Leonard (HL08740301)

THIS MAN (Jeremy Camp)
Available in the songbook "Restored"
Hal Leonard (HL 00306701)

WE (Joy Williams)
Available in the songbook "Genesis"
Brentwood-Benson Music Publishing (4575711307)

WELCOME HOME (YOU) (Brian Littrell)
Available in the songbook "Welcome Home"
Hal Leonard (HL00306830)

WHAT IF (Nichole Nordeman)
Available in the songbook "Brave"
Hal Leonard (HL00306729)

WHO I AM HATES WHO I'VE BEEN (Relient K)
Available in the songbook "MMHMM"
Hal Leonard (HL00690779)

WITHOUT YOU (Big Daddy Weave)
Available in the songbook "What I Was Made For"
Word Music (080689 502286)

WOW RECORDINGS & SONGBOOKS
Currently Available from the WOW Series

WOW HITS 2007
CD: Sparrow Records
(SPD67196)
Songbook: Word Music
(080689519284)

WOW HITS 2006
CD: Sparrow Records
(SPD11247)
Songbook: Word Music
(080689509285)

WOW HITS 2005
CD: Sparrow Records
(SPD71106)
Songbook: Word Music
(080689491283)

WOW HITS 2004
CD: Sparrow Records
(SPD90652)
Songbook: Word Music
(080689467288)

WOW HITS 2003
CD: Sparrow Records
(SPD39776)
Songbook: Word Music
(080689449284)

WOW HITS 2002
CD: Sparrow Records
(SPD51850)
Songbook: Word Music
(080689422287)

WOW HITS 2001
CD: Sparrow Records
(SPD1779)
Songbook: Word Music
(080689388286)

WOW 2000
CD: Sparrow Records
(SPD1703)
*Songbook:
Word Music*
(080689381287)

WOW 1998/1999
CD: Sparrow Records
(1999: SPD1686 / 1998: SPD1629)
Songbook: Word Music (includes all of
the songs from WOW 1998 and WOW 1999)
(080689380280)

WOW 1996/1997
CD: Sparrow Records
(1997: SPD1562 / 1996: SPD1516)
Songbook: Word Music (includes all of
the songs from WOW 1996 and WOW 1997)
(080689379284)